"An empower. *from Money* ( between our inner beliefs and our financial reality. It skillfully illustrates how a change in our thoughts and energy around money can lead to lasting transformation. A must-read for anyone seeking financial well-being with a soulful perspective."

—**Lynne Twist**, author of *The Soul of Money* and *Living a Committed Life*

"After a lifetime of reporting, talking, and writing about money, I realize Ellen has added the essential extra ingredient — the soul of money! And that makes every aspect of financial planning work smoothly."

—**Terry Savage**, *Chicago Tribune* Financial Columnist and author of *The Savage Truth on Money*

"I absolutely love the way *Messages from Money* invites us to deepen our relationship with money in an ingenious, personal way. If you're looking to increase your prosperity, this book needs to be on your list."

—**Kate Northrup**, bestselling author of *Money: A Love Story*

"*Messages from Money* is a delightful revelation! Ellen Rogin masterfully combines the art of abundance with practical financial know-how. Reading this book feels like discovering a treasure chest full of wisdom about both money and happiness."

—**Marci Shimoff**, #1 NY Times bestselling author of *Happy for No Reason* and *Chicken Soup for the Woman's Soul*

"In *Messages from Money*, Ellen Rogin takes our understanding of prosperity consciousness to an entirely new level. Taking the viewpoint and 'feelings' of money is a unique take on a concept that truly affects every aspect of one's life. After all, our relationship with money is exactly that — a relationship. And like any relationship, it is only healthy to the degree that we understand it, honor it, and treat it as 'it' would like to be treated. Plain and simple, this book is brilliant, and anyone fortunate enough to read it and embrace her wisdom will find themselves living a life of prosperity, peace, and happiness. Buy a copy of this book for everyone you love and care about. They will 'abundantly' thank you!"

—**Bob Burg**, coauthor of *The Go-Giver*

"Ellen has captured the essence of having a relationship with money, treating it like a friend, and making sure it loves you back. Now all you have to do is ask!"

—**Ken Honda**, author of *Happy Money: The Japanese Art of Making Peace with Your Money*

"This is far from your typical financial book. Every page felt like comfort food for my Soul. Both practical and spiritual, *Messages from Money* offers a revolutionary approach to building wealth and creating a heart-centered, prosperous life. I absolutely loved this book. You will too."

—**Barbara Huson** (formerly Stanny), author of *Rewire for Wealth* and *Overcoming Underearning*

"*Messages from Money* unveils a transformative approach to finances. Ellen shows us what's beyond the numbers. It's how we interact with money—how we talk to and judge ourselves with money, and how we appreciate money have more to do with financial wellness than we might imagine. And, Ellen reveals easy ways to shift our money attitudes. An inspiring guide for anyone seeking a more successful and less stressful connection with their financial journey."

—**Spencer Sherman**, MBA, Founder of Abacus, Creator of Dharma of Money & The Mindful Advisor Retreat

"*Messages from Money* masterfully delves into the intricate dance between our emotions and finances. Ellen Rogin's unique blend of practical wisdom and heartfelt guidance creates a roadmap for readers to stress less, prosper more, and find true abundance. If you're seeking a fresh perspective on achieving financial well-being, this book is a game-changer."

—**Matt Church**, Founder of Thought Leaders and author of *The Leadership Landscape*

"In *Messages from Money*, Ellen Rogin explores the deep-rooted beliefs and emotions surrounding our finances. This book is a heartfelt invitation to reshape your money mindset and create a life of greater abundance and fulfillment. With its compassionate insights and actionable advice, *Messages from Money* has the potential to spark a positive transformation in the way we relate to money."

—**Yasmin Nguyen**, author of *The Game of Joy*

# Messages
*from*
# Money

# Messages
*from*
# Money

## HOW TO STRESS LESS, PROSPER MORE, AND RESHAPE YOUR RELATIONSHIP WITH MONEY

## Ellen Rogin

First published in 2023 by Two Tango Productions

Production Consultant: Hambone Publishing
Publishing Consultant: AuthorPreneur Publishing Inc.

Editing by Mish Phillips, Emily Stephenson and Felicity Harrison
Cover design by Zizi Iryaspraha Subiyarta
Typesetting and interior design by David W. Edelstein
Author photo by Margo Popio

For information about this title, contact:

Ellen Rogin
ellen@ellenrogin.com
www.ellenrogin.com

ISBN 978-0-9815181-4-5 (paperback)
ISBN 978-0-9815181-5-2 (ebook)
ISBN 978-0-9815181-6-9 (audiobook)

*To all who are open to the possibility
of a generous and kind path with Money
and are committed to using it as a force
for good in the world.*

# Contents

## PROSPERITY PRACTICES

# Foreword

*Hi! People call me Money. I prefer you think of me as a loving friend who wants the best for you. It's funny how, over the many years I've been part of human life, people have attached all sorts of meaning to me. They've used me to control. They've used me to feel better about themselves. They've used me to feel important and worthy. Having lots of me makes some people feel more important; others feel I corrupt. Some of you use me to help others or to do enjoyable, meaningful things. Many of you worry I'll leave you. That there won't be enough of me. All of this is true and none of this is true. I am a mirror – a reflection of your inner world and of the outer world.*

*I have a secret for you: I am a force for good. I want you to be happy, healthy, and prosperous (though I know it doesn't always feel like that). Some of you hate me, some of you love me. Some of you think you don't deserve me, and others feel they are entitled to me.*

*What I most want is for us to have a great relationship. I want to be your friend. As a good friend, I'll be there for you. I won't enable, but I'll support you. And, as in any solid relationship, you'll have to do your part too.*

*What does that mean?*

*It means that you won't talk badly about me. Some people have said, "I hate money." Why would I want to hang around you if you hate me? Others want nothing to do with me and delegate our relationship to someone else: "Oh, my advisor (or wife, or partner, or accountant) will take care of it." How long would your friendships last if you pushed them off on someone else to nourish? I'm not saying others can't be involved – this may be the best thing for us – but don't ignore me, please.*

*Are you someone who constantly worries about me? Like an overprotective parent who's afraid something bad will happen, or a clingy, jealous partner who's afraid of being dumped? This isn't cool. When you hang on to me so tightly, it doesn't work well for either of us.*

*Ours is not a high-maintenance relationship. I appreciate you being aware that we are connected. If you are clear on what you want, I'll find it easier to be there for you. I care for you, and I want you to care for me. I also appreciate it when you share me generously. There is more than enough of me to go around if people decide to use me well.*

*I'm writing this book with Ellen. She and I have been having conversations for a while now. I would love to talk with you as well. Throughout the book, we'll explore ways in which you and I can communicate more clearly and easily with each other.*

*But why now? Why another money book? Why is this important? I have messages to share with you. I'm sharing them all the time, but many people aren't listening. When you take a moment to be quiet and are open to hearing them, you will receive messages from me that will help you feel more calm and guide you to create a life of prosperity on purpose.*

*Now, more than ever, I want to be there for you. We are on the precipice of important and inspired changes. We can continue to ruin our earth, create greater disparity and war... or we can use me as a tool for positive change. I like the sound of the latter. When conscious people use me as a force for good in the world, the ripple of positive impact is far-reaching. But many don't see this impact – they don't see beyond themselves. I see you and like-minded others waking up wanting to make a difference in the world, and I want to support you. I see you sharing your money for generous purposes; this is great, and there is more! When you acknowledge the ways in which you use me as a reflection of your values, our rippling impact will strengthen and stretch even further.*

*Please remember, we are partners for good. The fact that you found and chose to read this book lets me know you are ready to bring more of me into your life.*

*I'm excited! Giddy-up, let's get started!*

# Introduction:
# I Talk to Money

## Do You Talk to Money? Perhaps You Should.

Wouldn't it be cool if you could talk to your money and see what it has in store for you? Like having a Bat Phone to prosperity!

If you had told me when I started my career that I'd be *channeling* messages from Money, I wouldn't have even begun to understand what you were talking about. It still feels a bit weird to me even now.

For most of my professional career, I've worked in the 'left-brain' world of numbers, analytics, projections, and investments. I started as an auditor with a huge accounting firm, then headed into the field of wealth management, where I worked with people to help them reach their financial goals. For more than 25 years, I ran a successful financial advisory firm outside of Chicago, which I ultimately sold. I have lots of letters after my name and degrees to match this part of my professional background.

In the traditional settings of economics, investments, and money, I always felt something important was missing, but didn't know what. I sensed there was more at play when it came to money than most people talked about. After founding my financial advisory firm in my twenties, I became fascinated by how my clients related to money – their money personalities, financial decision-making, attitudes, and beliefs about money.

As an advisor, I could sense if someone was going to be on track with their goals without needing to know much at all about the specifics of their financial situation. I would listen to how a client talked about their goals and their life, and I'd *just know*. Of course, I backed up this 'knowing' with projections and financial planning. The numbers always confirmed what I thought.

A few years ago, I decided that I wanted to shift my career to do more public speaking, writing, coaching, and consulting (both within and outside of the financial services industry). Around the time I decided to leave my practice, I had a life-changing experience.

## I Talk to Money, and Money Talks Back

I was at a speaker and author workshop and the facilitator, Gary Stuart, led us through a partnered activity to work on tapping into our intuition. One person from each pair was instructed to think about a goal they had relating to money. I stood behind my partner, James, with my hands on his shoulders while he thought about his money issue. When he turned around to face me, I delivered a message to him ... only the words that came out weren't mine.

Here's what I said:

"F—k you for thinking that you can't do good work in the world and have me around! Like you believe there's something not spiritual about me. That's not true. It makes me not want to be around you at all!"

James stopped me, pulled out a pendant he was wearing, and said, "Ellen, one of my clients gave this to me; it's the Patron Saint of Poverty." And then he took it off.

"Ohhh, I feel so much better now. Now I want to be with you," I said. Then, I stood next to him and held his hand to walk beside him.

I enjoy a good swear word, but I don't fling them at people I don't know. Saying "F—k you" to James was certainly not how I would talk in that professional setting. Money had spoken through me. This experience was wonderful and, at the same time, a lot for my CPA, CFP® brain to take in. Looking back, I understand that Money wanted this communication to get both of our attentions.

I was excited and curious to explore what had happened, hoping it wasn't a one-time occurrence. I asked friends if I could see if Money had messages for them too. And Money did. People found the messages accurate, informative, and affirming. Their business and personal views of money transformed. And, for many, the results were extraordinary. The messages that come through now rarely contain expletives and are always supportive and optimistic.

> This is what excites and motivates me and my work; the vision of a world where people see their money as a gift to be shared and a tool for positive change.

Several years later, I reconnected with James, who shared that since our experience, everything had changed for the financial better in his business. He was bringing in clients with ease and making money that he had only dreamed of earlier.

I've now worked with people around the globe to enhance their relationships with Money. Here's what I've seen over and over...

## Money Wants to Have a Great Relationship with Us

Money is an energetic force that is truly for good. People assign all sorts of meanings to it – some helpful and many unhelpful. Most have not explored their relationships with Money, so they carry a huge amount of financial dysfunction. This can show up as stress, strained relationships, staying in a job they hate, and shame around how they have or haven't dealt with their finances. There are also significant problems globally that could be helped if more people had healthy relationships with Money. They'd also be more willing to share their resources and care for those in need. This is what excites and motivates me and my work: the vision of a world where people see their money as a gift to be shared and a tool for positive change.

There are many books available that can assist people to be more financially literate. Understanding financial terms, concepts, and strategies is important.

> Money wanted this book to be in the world to help bring the "woo to work," if you will. To give specific tools for understanding your money and your beliefs about it, and for transforming your relationship with Money to get real-world results.

There are also books that explore prosperity consciousness; most of these focus on shifting from scarcity thinking to an abundance approach, which is also crucial. Money wanted this book to be in the world to help bring the "woo to work," if you will. To give specific tools for understanding your money and your beliefs about it, and to transform your relationship with Money to get real-world results.

Throughout this book, I'll share ideas, tools, and

strategies that will help to shift and transform how you relate to your money. You'll discover ways to clear money blocks that may have limited your success in the past, and you'll learn how to use your mind as a tool to unlock your prosperity-creating abilities. I'll also share many action steps to turn your vision into a reality.

## Transformation Is Possible

Over and over, I've witnessed people who are committed to their growth shift their relationships with Money for the better. As a financial advisor, I used to share tactical strategies for allocating resources, investing, and tax savings to help my clients reach their goals. And they often did. I now realize that subtle and significant shifts can occur through less traditional methods. Such shifts enable the other methods to work even more effectively. These are the practices I share in this book.

Look out for improvements in your thoughts about money – as well as your confidence, actions, and business – while you are reading this book (and in the weeks and months that follow). The shifts may be subtle or more dramatic. I'm often amazed by the stories of creating prosperity that I hear from those who have used these ideas.

## Money as My Co-Author

I've written two other books, both with wonderful co-authors. In this book, Money is my co-author. When I sit down to write, I often feel like the words on the paper are coming through me, not from me. Throughout this book, you'll receive messages that Money wants to make sure you hear to help you in your prosperity journey.

You'll also find *Money Mantras* throughout the book. These are affirmational declarations from Money. You can use these phrases as anchors to help clarify and stabilize your next steps when you feel old patterns or beliefs arise around your finances. My clients often express gratitude and joy when they learn their individual *Money Mantras*. I'm confident you'll find some here that speak directly to you.

You'll also learn how to have your own conversations with Money. Know that when I've walked participants in my workshops through such processes, they hear messages that are comforting and inspiring. You will too.

In the first section of the book, I share concepts that form the foundation for the strategies you'll learn in the second section. You'll discover your Money MO, which will help you to understand your own approach and those of others in your life. You'll learn about how your relationship with Money impacts every area of your life, and begin to identify places where you and money could work better together.

In Section Two, I share prosperity practices you can use to build a beautiful relationship with Money. I've created these with Money's guidance over my many years consulting with groups and individuals to grow their prosperity. They work.

The practices fit into a framework that is divided into four parts:

**Aware** – What you think and say to yourself about Money directly impacts your results.

**Clear** – The more clarity you have around your vision and desires, the easier it is for you to have a plan of action.

**Care** – Money wants you to care for it in practical ways by managing it well, spending it responsibly, and planning for your financial future.

**Share** – Being generous and kind with your financial resources will not only serve others – it will also positively impact your financial life.

This *Prosperity on Purpose Framework* will be helpful in both your personal financial life and your business life. You'll find fun and effective prosperity practices to experiment with within each of the four sections. Many of these practices are snack-size and can be completed in a few minutes; others will take more time. I hope you'll use them. If you want to feel better about Money and see results, taking inspired action is crucial.

This book is deliberately digestible in a short amount of time. I've seen people avoid learning and dealing with their money when it feels too difficult, boring, or complicated. As you read, you'll likely discover areas of your financial life that require your attention: areas that you need to look deeper into and learn more about. Listen to that nudge to explore. There are resources online and in other books to help educate you in these more technical areas. My last book, *Picture Your Prosperity*, includes detailed discussions on financial goal-setting, spending, saving, and investing, if these are areas you want to explore in more detail.

Reading this book is the first step in taking action to create more prosperity on purpose. Through consulting with hundreds of people, I've found that engaging in a conversation with Money spurs financial transformation. This book is the beginning of your conversation. My sincere hope is that you feel better while you read this and notice prompt positive shifts.

Find a comfortable spot, grab a cup of tea, and let's talk with Money.

# Section 1

## *What Money Wants You to Know*

## Chapter 1

# You and Money Are a Thing

*I would love to be your trusted business and life partner. Would you like that too? I am here for you; please know this to be true. Trust, baby, trust!*

**— Money**

### You Are in a Relationship with Money

My mom used to talk about people who were dating by saying, "They're a thing." Usually, this meant they were happy and doing well together.

You and Money are a thing. You have a relationship with Money (whether you are conscious of it or not).

Money flows through every part of your life. You have beliefs about what is possible financially, how Money should work, and what it should and shouldn't be used for. You talk about Money (or never talk about it). When you think about Money, I bet it brings up feelings, emotions, or a reaction of some type.

Have you ever been with a couple where one person is always talking badly about the other one in front of them? Maybe they are hyper-critical or disparaging. I don't know about you, but this makes me feel very uncomfortable. And it makes me think worse of the complaining partner.

> What if you look at your money relationship as if it were a friendship or a romantic relationship; how would you be doing? Are you being a good partner? Are you caring and supportive? Are you distrustful and fearful? Would you want to hang around you if you were Money?

What if you look at your money relationship as if it were a friendship or a romantic relationship; how would you be doing? Are you being a good partner? Are you caring and supportive? Are you distrustful and fearful? Would you want to hang around you if you were Money?

How are you talking about your money to yourself and others? Do you say things like:

"I really wish someone else would deal with you."

"You cause all sorts of problems for people."

"If I just had more of you, everything would be better."

"I don't trust you to be there for me."

"You're too complicated for me. I just don't get you."

If you said these things often to your partner, how long do you think they'd hang around? What if, instead, you worked on your money relationship and added more awareness, clarity, caring, and generosity?

In a program I led with a small group of wealthy women, one of the attendees – we'll call her Julie – had come through a very difficult financial period. Not long ago, she had divorced and barely had funds to pay her rent. More recently, Julie had started a new business that was doing well. She was in a new relationship with a great guy. When we were discussing our feelings about Money, she said, "I hate Money!" Though she had been through a very stressful and tough time, I found this hatred jarring; it seemed to me like Money really came through for her. Yet she held deep resentment toward Money.

> Whether you believe you can talk to Money as I do, or not, it's a helpful metaphor.

Imagine if, in her new dating life, she consistently said to her boyfriend: "I hate you!" He may or may not stick around, and clearly, talking this way isn't building a strong relationship. Money tells me it loves when people speak nicely of it and are grateful. Julie would feel more financial peace if she fostered love and appreciation around her dealings with Money.

Whether you believe you can talk to Money as I do or not, it's a helpful metaphor.

We anthropomorphize money all the time when we say things like:

"Make your money work hard for you."

"Make sure your money lives as long as you do."

"Don't be a slave to money."

Are you a good partner to Money? Do you show up for Money, take care of it, and respect it? Or are you more of a user – you want it to be there for you when you need something, and otherwise you ignore it. Or maybe you are smothering in your relationship with Money, focusing so intently on it that much of your time and attention is spent managing, tracking, and thinking about it. Perhaps you just hope someone else will take care of Money for you, and you ignore it all together.

I was an economics major in college. We learned that money is a medium of exchange and that people are rational decision-makers. There's been lots of research since then in the field of behavioral finance, exploring how people think about and make decisions about money. People are anything but rational when it comes to their money.

For example, Duke University Professor and author Dan Ariely talks in his book, *Predictably Irrational*, about how people will drive 15 minutes to save $7 on a $25 pen but won't make the same drive to save $7 on a $455 suit.

Many times, people are just plain goofy when it comes to financial decisions. Why else would they spend all their assets on legal fees, fighting with their spouse during a divorce? Or spend more money than is coming in on designer clothes and eating out? Goofy!

Your relationship with Money will influence your personal relationships, income potential, investment results, and overall well-being. In this book, you'll learn how to befriend Money. When you do, it's more likely to show up for you when you need it, to support you, and to be a source of good in your life.

## Your Money Relationship Impacts Your Relationships

Many couples fight about money. I know you know that. But our feelings about Money can impact our relationships in less obvious ways as well.

When my mother was alive, we used to eat together every Sunday night. When we first started this, she felt compelled to take my husband, our kids, and me out for dinner. Then, our Sunday night dinners stopped abruptly. She was suddenly unavailable. After a few weeks, I asked her if she wanted to have dinner with us, and she blurted out, "I can't afford to keep taking you out to dinner each week!" She stopped seeing her grandkids because she was worried about money and didn't talk to me about her concerns. After that, we invited her to our house for Sunday night dinners. It's important to note, knowing about her financial situation, she actually *could* afford to take us out. We didn't expect it. We enjoyed having her at our house. But she let her money anxiety impact her relationships. In her case, these worries were not based in reality.

How do you feel when your friend orders a steak at dinner while you have a salad, and then she wants to split the bill? How do you feel when your friend itemizes the bill and prorates the tip based on what each person orders? Are you jumping at the chance to dine out with them again? There isn't a right or wrong here. There's a lack of talking about what makes you feel comfortable and judging where your friend is when it comes to money.

In marriages and partnerships, money obviously plays a big role. It's almost like an extra in-law. Each of you has your own relationship with Money, and it may be loving, or it may be stressful.

The more you understand and appreciate your money beliefs and those of your partner, the better. A lot of discord comes from being critical about how your honey approaches money as opposed to seeing the ways you complement each other.

How are your money beliefs developed? Much of how we view our money is based on what we saw and heard growing up. Whether you witnessed lots of fighting about money, ignoring it, spending it when there was none, getting everything you desire, or really not having enough, it's made a mark on you. Mix early experiences in with other money events in your life (like losing a job, having money stolen by a trusted person in your life, or coming into a windfall), all of which have an impact on how you relate to Money as an adult.

These marks show up in your attitudes and beliefs about Money. Most people are oblivious when it comes to knowing what they believe about Money. But being conscious of your money thoughts and beliefs can enhance what is working well for you and compensate for weaknesses in the ways you deal with money.

## Your Money Relationship Impacts Your Income

If you're self-employed, you might have felt weird when talking about your fees or charging appropriately. If you're negotiating a job, promotion, or raise, your relationship with Money is at play.

When someone asks how many siblings you have, what your phone number is, or how tall you are, there's typically no awkwardness about sharing these numbers (although I suppose it depends upon who's asking). But when asked what their fee is... many people stumble.

Some people are grounded in their ability to talk about fees and charging appropriately for their services. Others have built-in awkwardness around these discussions. It often comes down to the meaning they ascribe to their worth, or concern over the other person's needs or reactions.

Have you ever been offered a discount and thought, "That's cool, but I would have paid full price." I have. I gratefully accept the offer and have the feeling that they doubted their worth.

I'm not saying never to offer discounts or adjust your pricing; I'm suggesting that you evaluate your reasons for doing so.

During a Messages from Money session, Jennifer shared that she charged only a small monthly fee for her health coaching packages because she believed that people needed these services and wouldn't pay for them if they were more expensive. Money shared with her that by charging more, she'd actually be helping people commit to their health. The changes she was helping her clients make impacted their lives in such significant ways, the value they received was immense. A year after her session, Jennifer reported that she had created coaching packages that were at a five-times-greater monthly fee, she had many more clients, and her business had greater stability than it ever had before.

## Your Money Relationship Impacts Your Investment Results

Studies by Dalbar, Inc. consistently show that the average investor earns less than the market. Why? Because people often make investment decisions based on fear or greed. There's a tendency to feel that the markets will keep going in whatever direction they are going. People buy when stocks are high and sell their investments when markets are going down. Some people are also overconfident in their perception of what's going to happen in the markets. This is tricky business. Predicting market swings can't be done consistently.

When people focus too much of their attention on the increases and decreases in their investments, it can impact their results. Watching their value rise and fall can make people feel like they need to take some action, which is not always good for long-term performance and can be costly from a tax perspective. On the other hand, paying no attention to your investments won't serve you well either.

Money loves it when you look long-term, take care of it, and don't go crazy with risks.

## Financial Well-Being

Studies have shown that having strong relationships and close social ties can improve your health. Friends, romantic partners, family, and social connections can help you to reduce stress and heart-related risks.

Similarly, having a strong relationship with Money can improve your financial well-being. Financial wellness is your ability to meet your long-term needs, handle unexpected changes in the economy or your personal situation, and achieve your short- and long-term goals.

Most people talk about financial wellness starting with financial literacy, creating an emergency reserve, and getting out of debt. Of course, these are important, and more is needed. You can understand financial terms, be a disciplined saver and a savvy investor, and *still* be dysfunctional when it comes to Money.

Being great with money is much more than this. True financial well-being starts with a magnificent relationship with Money. I'll share many practices with you to enhance your financial well-being. The first step in this process is for you to recognize that you and Money are a thing, and that you want to transform your connection for the better.

## MESSAGE FROM MONEY

*I love being in a relationship with you. Can you trust this? For an even closer relationship, I appreciate it when you are kind and caring with me. I also love it when you give me attention, but not too much. I'm excited about building an even better, deeper connection with you. Please know that it can be easy and fun to work with me. Sometimes, you can be a bit too serious when you think of me. I know it can feel like work to care for me; it can also feel like joy!*

## Chapter 2

# We Need to Talk

*You know that expression, you catch more flies*
*with honey than with vinegar? It's like that with*
*me too. You catch more Money with honey! Please*
*remember to talk about me in loving ways. It*
*makes me feel good and I love to hang around with*
*people who make me feel good!*

**— Money**

Personal relationships flourish when communication is kind and supportive. This is true for your Money relationship as well. How aware are you of the ways you think and speak about Money and your financial situation? Deliberate and compassionate words about Money will bring you closer to it.

## Abracadabra

I've always loved the idea of magical abilities. Mary Poppins, Samantha Stephens (if you know, you know), and Hermione Granger inspire me. I love to imagine singing, wiggling my nose, or waving a wand to clean my house, cook meals, or even attract new business.

Do you know what *abracadabra* means?

It has Hebrew and Aramaic roots which translate to: "I create as I speak."

Your words are powerful. Changing your language could change your behavior and results. In their book, *Words Can Change Your Brain*, Andrew Newberg, M.D. and Mark Robert Waldman discuss how just saying the word "peace" (out loud or in your head) can boost your sense of peacefulness. When we say "peace," the brain responds by triggering pleasure chemicals like dopamine to be released, which reduces anxiety and relaxes the body. By saying "peace", we create peace – abracadabra!

Words are magical. What are you saying about your money? About your ability to manage and earn money? About the business world? Your words matter.

Money doesn't like it when you talk badly about it. Who would?

If you were always criticizing your partner, would they stick around? If they did, your relationship would not be very loving or strong. What are you saying about Money? Do you catch yourself saying any of the following?

"I suck when it comes to money."

"Money makes people do bad things."

"I'm great at making money, but not good at keeping it."

"I wish someone else would just take care of my money for me."

"Managing money is hard."

"I'm just not good at making money."

"I hate talking about fees."

*Abracadabra* – I create as I speak. What are you creating when it comes to your money?

> Remember, you and Money are a thing. Choose your words consciously, carefully, and kindly.

Do you remember that game with fortune-cookie messages? The one where you add "in bed" after you read the fortune? What if you changed the phrases above to replace "money" with "him" or "her"? Remember, you and Money are a thing. Choose your words consciously, carefully, and kindly.

In the second half of this book, you'll find many *Money Mantras*. These are opportunities to exercise the creative power of your words with positive expressions. You can repeat these mantras to focus on your money relationship with optimism and support.

*When you speak of me in positive and supportive
ways, it makes me feel closer to you. If you use kind
words as you think and talk about me, I know you'll
feel better about me too. It is more than okay to
have loving thoughts about our relationship. Loving
Money. Loving Money. Loving Money.*

**— Money**

## Money Wants More Than a Hook-Up

Are you someone who values your relationship with Money or do you only care about it when you need something? A good relationship requires caring on both sides. No one likes a user. Including Money.

> Money loves to be cared for. Money loves to be respected. Money is happy to be there for you. Please don't ignore it.

Money loves to be cared for. Money loves to be respected. Money is happy to be there for you. Please don't ignore it.

On the other hand, Money doesn't love it when you're a clingy, jealous partner. Do you find yourself hanging on so tightly to Money that you're afraid to spend or share it? I'll share suggestions in Section Two for you to take smart actions that show Money you care about it.

## What's Your Money MO?

Each of us has a Money *modus operandi*. This is how we approach Money in our lives and in our relationships. It may impact how you and your partner connect or conflict around Money. Let's explore what yours might be.

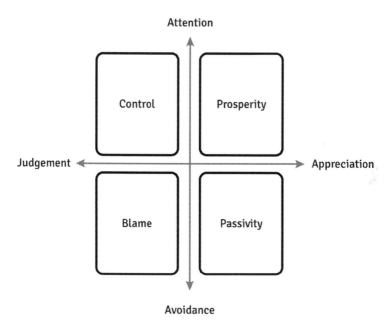

Think about where you fall on the *judgment* versus *appreciation* scale when it comes to Money. Are you someone who tends to judge how others are around Money? Do you spend energy assessing how they spend, value, earn, and save their money? These

might be people you work with, live with, are friends
with, or just know of. Perhaps you feel judged by
others when it comes to how you handle your money.
Or maybe you spend a lot of time beating yourself up
around how you are with Money.

On the other hand, perhaps you sit in a place of
appreciation for others regarding how they handle
Money. You see that everyone is on their own journey
and makes their own decisions. You may choose a different path, but you don't spend your time judging
others. You might be someone who swims in a sea
of gratitude for what you have and how others support you.

It's also helpful to look at where you fall on
the *attention* versus *avoidance* scale with Money.

Typically, more attention is good, but (as is often
the case) there can be a shadow side. Too much attention can turn extreme and unhelpful. Imagine living
with someone who ranks highly on attention and high
on judgment. They might fall into the controlling cat-
egory. It might be challenging to talk about finances
when you're feeling judged by this person. Or maybe
you're the controlling one and wonder why you argue
so much with your partner about Money. You may
think, "If they understood more about finances, they'd
realize I was right!" Can you step into your partner's
shoes and consider how they might feel when you talk
with them about money?

What if your avoidance and appreciation levels are high? You might be very happy to have your partner or advisor handling financial matters for you. This may work for a while, but your passivity could ultimately end up with you being unprepared to deal with your money if that person is no longer able to manage your finances for you. Or you could find yourself in a situation where you've been taken advantage of by someone you'd indiscriminately trusted.

If your attention and appreciation levels are high, your MO tends toward prosperity. Cool, right? You can use this position to support and inspire people you care about to join you. Ask yourself, "If something happened to me, would those I love and care for be able to manage financially?"

Take a moment to mark where you believe you are on the Money MO chart. Where are other people in your life? Now consider where you would *like* to be.

Your Money MO is not permanent like a bad tattoo; it's certainly changeable. You can move to a place of more appreciation and attention. Money would love to see you do just that! In Section Two, you'll find plenty of prosperity practices to help you be more deliberately appreciative and attentive. This will enhance your Money relationship.

## Chapter 3

# Going with the Current or Against

*Please don't try to swim against the current.
Prosperity is a flow, and you can let it
carry you. Or you can fight it with doubts,
fears, and misaligned beliefs.*

**— Money**

## Blocks to True Prosperity

In 2017, my husband Steven competed in an Ironman competition. If you're unfamiliar, an Ironman is a triathlon on steroids. Swim 2.4 miles, bike 112 miles, then… run a marathon. Steven is a good swimmer, but he did much better than he'd expected to in the swim portion of the race. Part of the reason he did so well was that he was swimming down the Ohio River. Swimming with the current propelled him and greatly shortened his swim time. If they'd had to swim against the current, the results would have been very different.

When it comes to Money, it's common to swim against the current (making things more difficult and less fun). How? By focusing on the wrong things. By swimming in the waters of scarcity thinking.

With a scarcity focus, we experience restrictive feelings such as worry, blame, and envy. The feelings triggered by scarcity thinking are the same ones most people get when they hear the words *diet* or *budget*.

Going with the current is about an attitude of abundance. It involves a focus of collaboration, celebration, and positivity. When you are going with the current, you believe there is more than enough to go around. You see challenges as redirection and learning opportunities. Going with the current is based on generosity. It feels expansive, optimistic, and full of possibility.

Let's explore the eight ways in which scarcity-thinkers tend to go against the current. I'll also unpack how each of these common tendencies can be counteracted so that you can optimize your energy and flow with the current.

### 1. Worrying

Worry is not a financial strategy. Scarcity is fear-based. But many people worry about what could happen in the future; the chatter in our heads can sound like:

"What if I lose my job? What if I lose it all? What

if this deal falls apart? What if the markets plummet? What if my brilliant kid gets into Harvard – how am I going to pay for that? What if I end up homeless?"

These worries can be realistic for some people. But for many, they are manufactured.

Worrying about your money is like swimming against a rip current. It makes everything feel scarier and takes more time. It's danger-

> Worry can cause you to make illogical decisions about your money, your business, and your financial future.

ous. Flailing and pushing feels like a productive thing to do, but it's exhausting and counterproductive. Money tells me all the time that people shouldn't worry about it. It's not that financial challenges don't come up for people. They do. It's that the process of worrying doesn't help.

In their book *Scarcity: Why Having Too Little Means So Much*, researchers Sendhil Mullainathan and Eldar Shafir share that when people are freaked out about their money and their backs are up against the wall, their IQ can actually drop. Worry can cause you to make illogical decisions about your money, your business, and your financial future.

**Marie**

For over two decades, Marie ran a small consulting practice. Her income was stable but not at the level she wanted. She was stressed and a bit bored with her work. Marie was juggling a lot: caring for her daughter who has learning difficulties, being a good wife and friend, and serving her clients. She was afraid to invest money in her business. Marie shared a member of the firm's support staff, but they weren't a good fit. She found him "toxic", yet she was afraid to let go of him and get her own assistant. During our consultation, the message Marie received from Money was that her income could double in a few years. When she heard this, Marie knew it was true. Grounded in this vision of what was possible, her fear began to dimin-ish. New ideal clients started flowing into her business. She let go of the toxic member of support staff and found a perfect new assistant.

> **When you get to the other side of worry, prosperity is often waiting for you.**

By releasing her worry about Money in her business, Marie became busier than ever. Not only is she now making more money, she's also loving her work again.

It is possible to move through money anxiety to a place of calm. I'll share tools in Section Two to help you move from fear to clear when you start to feel afraid. When you get to the other side of worry, prosperity often awaits you.

## 2. Story Telling

We all make up stories in our heads. Even if you don't consider yourself to be creative, it's quite possible that you're playing the imagination game, conjuring up images of what will happen in the future. If we're not deliberate in our story crafting, we can often wind up writing horror films rather than fairy tales.

We can't know what the future will bring. Yes, there is always uncertainty. But there is also opportunity.

Once, I remember quickly reading an email from a client who was asking about his portfolio. I read that he was upset

> We can't know what the future will bring. Yes, there is always uncertainty. But there is also opportunity.

about what was happening. I quickly crafted a scenario: he was going to fire me and move his money to another advisor. I spent all weekend crafting a response to his email and worrying about our relationship. Before hitting send on my response, I re-read his original email. He had merely asked a question. The response I'd written didn't even answer the question he'd asked, and could have caused big issues.

When someone doesn't return a call, we might craft a story as to why: "They are mad at me," or, "They don't want to work with me; that's the only reason they ghosted me." Most often, they simply got busy.

We just aren't as important as we'd like to think we are in the lives of our clients and prospects!

Rob S. was a prospect I had for a consulting project, who had stopped returning my emails. I was about to give up on the relationship when I emailed him with a meeting notice by mistake. I'd meant to send the notice to Rob R., and I instead sent it to Rob S. He emailed me back immediately to say that the proposed meeting date wouldn't work for him, but how about another time? As it turned out, his wife had been ill, his energy had been focused on her, and that's why he hadn't responded.

The story that Rob didn't want to work with me was one I'd crafted. By conjuring up such a tale, I was going against the current.

Remember, words matter. Our psychological reaction to stories and fantasies is very similar to our psychological reaction to other inputs from our senses (such as smells, tastes, and images). Your brain doesn't register the difference between reality and imagination; when you imagine a scary situation, it's perceived as an actual threat. When you imagine safety, your brain believes that you are safe.

So, if you're going to make up a story, why not make up a good one?

### 3. Clinging and Grasping

Are you a bit clingy when it comes to your money? Going against the current often means grasping for money. Even if you have lots of financial resources, it's easy to want more and more. You might think, "What's so wrong with that?" It's wonderful to desire and have a plan for growing your money, especially if you have uses for it based on your values. I'm referring to the feelings of grasping for and clinging to your desire for more.

The word "want" is a synonym of the word "lack." When you focus your attention on wanting, you become more aware of what you lack rather than of what you actually desire Money to do for you. It's much more effective to shift your focus from wanting Money to welcoming Money into your life.

> The word want is a synonym of the word lack. When you focus your attention on wanting, you become more aware of what you lack rather than of what you actually desire Money to do for you. It's much more effective to shift your focus from wanting Money to welcoming Money into your life.

Imagine a friendship in which you demand a lot. You expect your friend to drop everything whenever you feel like seeing her and to help you no matter what you need. You spend a lot of your energy trying to get her to do more and more. It feels uncomfortable, right? Money doesn't like it either. This grasping comes from a scarcity focus.

Welcoming Money into your life means making

space for it and having a plan for allocating it well and taking care of it. With this welcoming energy, you can move from going *against* to going *with* the current.

**Kim**

During our first session together, Kim heard loud and clear that Money wanted her to stop hanging on so tightly.

She was going out for dinner with her husband the evening after our session; they hadn't been on a date in a while. She looked through her closet for something to wear and found only old clothes that didn't make her feel special. She hadn't bought anything new in a long time because she was worried about having enough money for their son's college and daughter's activities. Kim threw on an old black top and jeans.

When they got home from dinner, Kim said, "F—k this!" She and her husband had been great savers for their kids' educations, she was doing well in her coaching business, and she realized this scarcity energy wasn't going to move them ahead. She thought, "I know Money and I are good," and went online to buy new clothes.

The following Monday, Kim heard a story on the radio about a special tax break the government was offering. She reached out to her accountant to see if she and her husband were eligible. Her accountant informed her that if they filled in the necessary forms before the quickly approaching

deadline, they would get a $2,000 tax refund…
which they did. The day after that, she found out
that they were due a credit on the bus fees they
had been paying the school district. Coincidence?

Kim knows that by letting her fear of not having
enough go, she opened the flow to this unexpected
money. She moved from going against to going
with the current, with immediate results.

### 4. Blaming Money

Money is not your problem. Period.

Having more financial wealth might help solve
your problem. Then again, it might not. With more
money, you might just have different issues. Either
way, Money isn't the issue.

If you are spending more than comes in, it's not
Money's fault. If you are fighting with your partner
about finances, it's not Money's fault. If you worry
all the time that you won't have enough, it's not
Money's fault.

It can feel good to have someone to blame when
problems occur, and the blame may be justified, but
it never improves the situation. Blame is like sugar. It
feels great for a short time, but ultimately leaves you
depleted of energy and feeling lousy.

Money tells me all the time that it doesn't like
people blaming it for their issues. No one likes to
be falsely accused. I remember when our kids were

young, and our son Benjy got blamed for scratching the wooden end of our bed – we assumed it was his fault. We later found out that it was his two-year-old sister Amy who had decided it would be fun to gnaw on the bedpost. Benjy was upset, understandably. Have you been blaming Money for hurt relationships, stress in your life, or something else? If there's a financial issue you have that you're blaming Money for, consider if this is really helping. Spoiler alert! It's not. Accusing Money for your issues is like blaming the gym for the fact that you ate an entire tub of ice cream. Or pointing the finger at the highway from your old crappy car.

Money is like a professional chef's knife: it can help you or hurt you, depending on how you use it.

Money is not inherently evil. It's also not your savior. Can more money ease situations and offer solutions? Of course it can. But if you believe that having all the money you think you'd ever want would cause all of your issues to disappear, you're mistaken.

Many years ago, I met a couple who won a significant amount of money in the lottery. Did winning this money help their situation? Yes, it did. They had five kids and lived in a dilapidated rental home. The money enabled them to buy a new home and easily feed and clothe their family. But they also experienced stress they hadn't expected. When I spoke with Anna about their situation, she said, "Ellen, everyone thinks it's so great to be a lottery winner, but I've never been more worried. This money has caused so many problems for us." And then she began to cry. Anna and her husband Jesse had never had much money; they had a lot to learn. Money wasn't the problem; instead, their work was around learning, planning, and deliberately creating healthy money beliefs to build a healthy relationship with Money. Sadly, as is the case with many people who experience windfalls, they didn't do the work needed or get the right support: within a decade, they had very little money left.

What if you were to see Money as your partner instead? Would you show up differently in your relationship with it? Going with the current is about learning ways to positively grow your relationship with Money.

### 5. Being Materialistic

There's nothing wrong with enjoying nice things. It's the motivation behind your purchases that determines if you are going with the current or against it.

Maybe you can relate to the 'Sex in the City' character Carrie Bradshaw's comment, "I like my money right where I can see it – hanging in my closet!" That's cool if your clothes bring you joy and help you to express yourself. But dressing merely to impress and accumulating possessions to make yourself feel more important are signs you're going against the current. In fact, research suggests that materialistic people are less happy than their peers.

When you spend consciously based upon your

values, you're flowing with the current. Money loves to support you and doesn't like to be used carelessly. Who would?

Adding a gratitude practice to your daily routine can help reduce materialistic tendencies. I'll share simple ways to do this in Section 2. Practicing gratitude is a beautiful way to begin to move with the current and build your prosperity.

### 6. Keeping Secrets

Do you have money secrets? In a survey by Forbes, 31 percent of people reported having some type of financial infidelity. It might be hidden credit card debt, hiding shopping bags in the trunk of your car or the back of your closet, or paying with cash so your partner can't trace where you're spending. There are many ways financial deception can show up.

Keeping secrets of any kind is awful for your relationships, and financial secret-keeping is a surefire way to go against the current. The energy you spend holding on to unshared financial issues will slow you down in big ways.

Josh

In a consultation with Josh, he shared that he hadn't told his wife about a real estate investment that was losing money and required him to add money each month to support the project. He wanted to shield her from the stress of their situation. This weighed heavily on Josh. With my encouragement, he shared the details of the real estate issues with his wife. She was supportive and offered potential solutions for the situation. Josh felt much lighter not having to hold on to this secret. With the help of his wife, they found a solution to get rid of this failing investment.

Coming clean about the skeletons in your money closet will help you to begin to find solutions to issues, pay down debts, and create space for prosperity in your life. We'll talk about how to care for your money in practical ways and make it easier to clean up financial messes that you may be hiding.

### 7. Being Judgy

It's easy to be judgmental about how others are with their money. We've all done it. Judgy thoughts can sound like:

"I cannot believe they would spend that much money on a handbag. That's ridiculous!"

"They're just trying to impress people by buying a crazy expensive car like that."

"I would never work all those hours and miss important events with my family just to earn more money."

"They are so cheap! I hate going out to dinner with them because they always split the bill by item."

No one likes to be judged. We often criticize others to protect from being criticized ourselves. And if you're fighting with your partner about finances, you're likely judging as opposed to appreciating how they are with money. Judgment also comes into play when other people's values aren't the same as yours. Being righteous won't make you prosperous. Everyone is on their own journey. Your negative opinions of how others handle Money will only block you from going with the current.

> Judgement also comes into play when other people's values aren't the same as yours. Being righteous won't make you prosperous. Everyone is on their own journey.

Perhaps you don't judge others, but instead put the negative attention on your past money mistakes. Money wants you to forgive yourself. Mistakes are ways to learn what not to do in the future.

Check in again on where you are on the judgement/appreciation scale using the Money MO chart in the previous chapter.

### 8. Envy

Envy is a huge contributor to going against the current. This is a resentful longing to have someone else's possessions, successes, or qualities.

You'll know you are swimming against the current when something awesome happens to someone you know, and instead of being excited for them, you either judge, resent, or criticize them. Alternatively, you may catch yourself beating yourself up for not achieving what they have.

The energy you spend wishing for what someone else has is a waste. It not only keeps you feeling resentful, but also robs creative energy that could be better used for moving your goals forward.

When you are going with the current, you are excited for the success of others. Practice celebrating other people's accomplishments and feeling genuinely thrilled for them rather than bad that you haven't achieved what you would like to. Their achievements are not your failures, but your opportunities to connect, celebrate, and learn.

If you catch yourself criticizing someone's success, pause to ask yourself why. Why spend your energy judging them? I remember having a lot of negative focus on a celebrity who talks about personal finances. She's on TV, she's written many books, and she gets lots of exposure. I would criticize her knowledge and judge her personality. When I spent time exploring why she bugged me so much, I realized that she was doing what I thought I should be doing more of: serving

> When you are going with the current, you are excited for the success of others. Practice celebrating other people's accomplishments and feeling genuinely thrilled for them rather than bad that you haven't achieved what you would like to. Their achievements are not your failures, but your opportunities to connect, celebrate, and learn.

people around their money issues. I came to appreciate that her audience was different to mine and the
advice she gives is valuable to the people she serves. I
moved from going against the current to flowing with
the current in my viewpoint on her. Letting go of my
judgments of her opened up more space for creativity.
Soon after this, I completed my first book, *Great with
Money*. It feels much better to appreciate someone
than to burn energy resenting them.

Aggressive competition is a cousin of envy. This
might show up as thoughts such as, "For me to win,
you have to lose," or, "There are only so many good
opportunities out there, so I'll make sure they go to
me and not you." People who operate from this space
may make a lot of money, but they don't make a lot
of friends. When you go with the current, it's possible
to do well financially *and* collaborate generously with
others. If you grow a reputation for being great to
work with, your work life will become easier and way
more enjoyable.

## Can You Go Against the Current and Still Make Money?

Many people go against the current and still have
financial success, but this doesn't mean they experience *true* prosperity. Think of the friends, family
members, or colleagues you have who make lots of

money but have failed relationships, bad health, stress, and experience loneliness. You may falsely believe that Money is the root cause of their problems – it's not. Issues typically arise from their beliefs around Money, such as what it takes to earn money and what their wealth says about them as a person.

There are lots of wealthy people who use their money as a force for good in the world. My passion is to inspire and support people to be in this camp. In the next section, I'll offer prosperity practices to help you create a beautiful Money relationship, and we'll explore actionable ideas to build prosperity on purpose. Get your paddles ready to go with the current!

# Section 2

## *Prosperity Practices*

## Chapter 4:

# The Create Prosperity on Purpose Framework

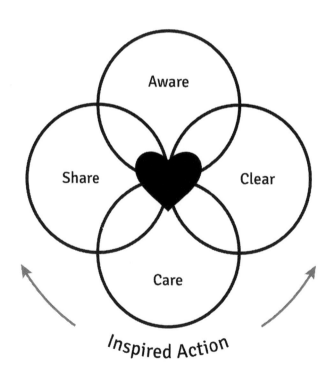

## The Recipe for Prosperity Pie

I love baking. I started as a little girl baking cookies with my mom. I also had an Easy Bake Oven as a child. It came with baking mixes where all I had to do was add water and pour the mixture into a small pan. I then put the pan in the toy oven (basically a light bulb), set a timer, and out would pop a little cake. Easy!

To this day, I find it fun to browse through cookbooks and online for new desserts to make. And I often go back to the same recipes I know my family loves. Having a recipe to follow provides me with a step-by-step plan of action.

In this section of the book, I share easy-bake prosperity practices. They are designed to help you in each of the four areas of the *Create Prosperity on Purpose Framework*.

There are four parts to the framework:

**Aware** – What you think and say about Money directly impacts your results. Being aware of your thoughts, noticing your words, and recognizing your feelings are all important aspects of transforming your relationship with Money for the better.

**Clear** – It's pretty darn hard to attain your goals if you don't know what they are. What do you want to create in your life? The more detailed your vision, the easier it is for you to have a plan of action.

**Care** – Money wants you to care for it in practical ways by managing it well, spending it responsibly, and planning for your financial future. It also wants to be cared for in energetic ways, such as being involved with it and aligning your approach with your values.

**Share** – Hanging on too tightly to what you have limits your flow of prosperity. Being generous and kind with your financial resources will not only serve others but will positively impact your financial life.

## The Ingredients

Action is the baking powder to your recipe. It's the active ingredient that makes your prosperity rise.

You'll find many suggestions for gaining traction through action in this section of the book. You will see better results when you experiment with the practices instead of merely reading them. The *Prosperity on Purpose Framework* is best approached in order: aware, clear, care, and then share.

> Action is the baking powder to your recipe. It's the active ingredient that makes your prosperity rise.

Some prosperity practices will likely speak to you and your style more than others will. Great! Work with those you think will best serve you. And I do encourage you to try the ones that bring up some resistance. You know that expression, *what you resist persists?* Perhaps the area you are avoiding is just the place you need to direct your focus.

I always avoided journaling. I tried it after reading Julia Cameron's book, 'The Artists Way.' She talked about writing morning pages to increase creativity. I had heard from several people how wonderful it was for them, so I gave it a try. It just wasn't for me. It felt annoying to sit and write, my hand hurt, and I eventually gave up.

Years later, I was working on a blog and did a search on "finding your purpose." I landed on a site that suggested to write the question: "What is my purpose?" and just start writing. Sitting in a Starbucks on Piedmont Avenue in Atlanta, I did just that on my laptop. After a minute or so, all sorts of cool realizations started showing up. It was as if ideas were dropping onto the page from above. It was easy. It was fun. I was hooked.

Since then, most days, I still use that prompt (and add other questions to it depending on what's going on for me). Journaling with a keyboard works better for me than writing by hand. It's faster and easier for me. I realized from this experience that by adjusting suggested practices to better suit me, I will get the results I'm looking for. This is like adding a little extra cinnamon to your baking because you love the flavor, or leaving out the nuts because you don't like the consistency.

Once I started to receive messages from Money, I realized that journaling was the easiest way for Money to talk to me. It's simple: I ask a question and type out the answers from Money.

You'll find journaling prompts in some of the following pages. If journaling isn't your jam, I get it. And perhaps you could give it a try and see what shows up for you.

Notice when you're avoiding a practice or deliberately deciding you don't need to work on an area as you've "already handled it." If you're avoiding it, okay: Why? Have you tried it in the past and it didn't work for you? Perhaps it's worth trying it again, as I did with journaling. If you feel yourself resisting, release any judgment and notice what's coming up for you. There is so much shame and judgment relating to how people deal with money – I'm not going to pile on more. When you approach these practices believing that you will find them effortless and fun, it will feel like easy-bake prosperity. I know that these activities can work. I suspect if you've read this far, you're game for giving them a try!

So, go ahead, read on, try out the practices, and bake your prosperity pie!

*Chapter 5*

# Aware

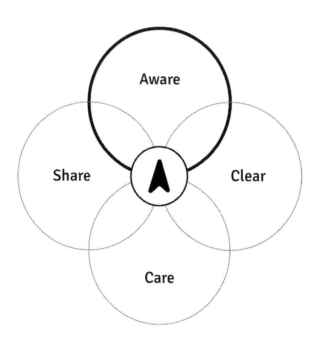

## Turn on the Financial Light

It's easier to create a great relationship with Money when you become aware of what you think and believe about it. It's like walking into a dark room and flipping on the light; suddenly, you can see more clearly and get where you want to go without slamming into anything.

What you think and say about your money has a huge impact on your results. The first step to improving your relationship with Money is to notice what you are thinking and saying to yourself.

When you start to pay attention to what you are thinking, saying, and believing about money, you'll begin to more easily recognize whether you're going with or against the current. You'll see what's holding you back and create what you desire with ease.

## Watch Your Words

What would happen if people knew what we were really thinking about them? Even toward the people we love the most, sometimes we have judgments, anger, mean intentions, and insecurities that sweep through our thoughts. They are often fleeting. Hopefully not expressed or persistent. But we do have them. You have these kinds of tapes playing in your head about money as well: about your relationship with Money, and about how others are with their money.

What if Money could hear you? Would you be creating the type of relationship you'd like to have with Money? Okay, you might think this is silly. How could *money* know what I was thinking about it or how other people deal with it?

Remember: *abracadabra* – I create as I speak. You're likely familiar with how magicians use this as an incantation. It is like magic. The more deliberately you think and use words about Money, the better relationship you'll create.

It's easy to get carried away in thoughts of worry and dread, especially when it comes to Money. But worry is a bad financial strategy. The feelings that come along with these limiting thoughts indicate that you're going against the current. These limiting thoughts can cloud your ability to see opportunities or find solutions, and they can even change how you see situations.

In a consultation, my client (we'll call her Josie) asked about a real estate investment that wasn't working out as she had planned. Money responded with a message asking about her original intent for the deal. Josie said that she had told her broker she was looking for an opportunity that was "too good to be true." As soon as she said that, I stopped her and said, "Well… that is exactly what you got, right?" Sometimes, you need someone else to put the spotlight on how you're talking about your financial goals and Money. Josie now realizes how her words create her reality and is more conscious of how she speaks about Money and her goals.

How do you become more aware of what money-related thoughts and words swirl around your head or fall out of your mouth?

By being more mindful. What does that mean? Mindfulness is simply about paying attention. Noticing without judgment what's happening in the present moment.

Try this right now. Look around the space you're in and notice something you haven't noticed for a long time, if ever before. Every time I do this in a room that I spend a lot of time in, I'm amazed at what I *don't* typically pay attention to.

With practice, you'll become more aware of your thoughts and beliefs about Money.

## MESSAGE FROM MONEY

*I appreciate it when you talk kindly about me behind my back. It's hurtful when you think I won't be there for you and you say mean things about me. It is even harder when you think and talk negatively of your ability to call me into your life and take care of me. I know you can be a great partner. Yes, you would benefit from learning more and having better habits, but I know we can create a wonderful relationship.*

## Gain Traction Through Action

Consider a concern you have about Money. Perhaps it's the current situation you're in, or a difficult financial situation you've experienced in the past. It could even be a worry you have about the future.

Take a moment to notice what you feel when you have that thought. Go ahead and truly feel that emotion. Where in your body do you feel it?

Quite often, when you experience an uncomfortable feeling about Money or your financial situation, there is a fear of something happening in the future, or regret and shame about something you did or didn't do in the past.

A future focus can be helpful; we'll talk about this more in Chapter Six. But worry and anxiety about what may or may not happen down the road is very rarely helpful. A small amount of concern may motivate some people. When you lose sleep, fight with your partner, or have constant anxiety about money issues, it is not.

As the French philosopher Michel de Montaigne said:

*"He who fears he shall suffer,*
*already suffers what he fears."*

According to a study by Penn State researchers Lucas LaFreniere and Michelle Newman, 91.4 percent of what people worry about doesn't come true.

Yet these worries can cause suffering and lead to bad financial decisions.

If your anxiety about money is severe and persistent, please seek professional help.

If your concerns are periodic, the following practice may help you.

When you notice a thought about something you don't want to happen or catch yourself saying something you don't want to show up for you, say: "cancel/clear away." Cancel the thought and replace it with something you prefer.

"I'll have to work until I die." Cancel/clear away.

"What if my investments go down to nothing?" Cancel/clear away.

"I'll probably lose my job, and then what?" Cancel/clear away.

"If interest rates go up next year, I'll lose my business." Cancel/clear away.

Could any of these worries come true? Sure. But spending time worrying about them now is taking energy away from finding solutions and creative ideas to deal with what could come up.

I'm not saying never think about anything that could go wrong. I'm saying don't spend your time worrying about it. Spend your time thinking about what you would prefer and how you'd solve problems if they did come up.

Michael Phelps, the Olympic swimmer, would not only visualize how he wanted his races to go, but also what he would do if something went wrong. If there was a rip in his swimsuit or water in his goggles, he knew how he would handle it. This strategy clearly paid off for him. He is now the most successful Olympic athlete ever, and this strategy helped him get there.

In the 2008 Olympics, Phelps was swimming the 200-meter fly when his goggles filled with water. He was swimming blind. Instead of freaking out or giving up, he started counting his strokes. He'd prepared for this. Not only did he win the gold, but he set a world record. Practicing preparedness helped him to win eight gold medals that year, the most golds won by anyone in any single Olympic Games.

We'll talk more in Chapter Six about the power of visualization.

## MONEY MANTRA

**My financial life is working out for the highest good of all.**

## Mindful Thoughts

When I was in graduate school, I had a roommate – we'll call her Margo – who never stopped talking. Thankfully, it was a temporary living situation. It drove me up the wall. Sometimes, I feel like I have a Margo living in my head when my thoughts don't stop.

Research out of Queen's University in Canada found that we have about 6.5 thoughts per minute. That's about 6,200 thoughts per day if we assume eight hours of sleep.

Our minds yap at us much of the time. It's easy to believe our thoughts. But just because you're thinking a thought doesn't mean it's true or helpful.

When we are in constant conversation with ourselves, especially if our chatter is negative, it's easy to miss what's right in front of us.

During the pandemic, my husband Steven and I were in Black Mountain, North Carolina, working remotely. Black Mountain is a lovely little town filled with cute shops, breweries, and restaurants. One night, Steven was visibly stressed about a project he was working on. As we walked down the street and past a gift shop, I said to him, "You should get this sign." He replied, "Why would you tell me to get a sign that says, 'Think about what could go wrong!'" I stared at him, confused, and then laughed and said, "Steven, look at the sign again." It actually read:

*Think About What Could Go Right.*

His worries and stressful thoughts hijacked his ability to accurately perceive what was right in front of him.

One way to quiet Margo down (or whatever you choose to name your inner annoying roommate) is through meditation. Research has indicated that a regular practice of mindfulness meditation can quiet the default mode network (the fancy name for the set of regions in the brain that are at play when Margo won't shut up).

What does meditation have to do with Money? It's more than likely that some of your 6,200 thoughts per day relate to Money (and such thoughts aren't always positive). Remember, just because you have a thought doesn't mean it is true; worries about your financial future don't mean that they will come to fruition. A regular meditation practice has helped me to notice my thoughts and be less hooked into them. It's shown me that simply having a thought doesn't mean it's true or helpful. My meditation practice has made it easier for me to let limiting thoughts pass by like cars driving past my house. I don't have to jump in those cars or spend time wondering about the make and model. With a calmer, quieter mind, I also find it easier to be more deliberate and think about helpful beliefs and to use my words to focus on what I desire (*abracadabra* – I create as I speak).

I have practiced meditation regularly for many years. Now, I can't *not* meditate each day. For me, not meditating would be like leaving the house without brushing my teeth. I've seen the benefits over time in terms of feeling calm, being more creative with problem-solving, and helping others around me to feel more relaxed as well. My meditation practice also has a huge positive impact on my business.

When my mind is quiet, I'm able to tap into my intuition. I'm able to hear my own good intentions. And I hear messages from Money more clearly.

Nikki has been in many of my workshops and worked with me to clear her money blocks and build out her business vision. She has been following my prosperity practices for a while now, and decided to incorporate small sessions of mindfulness meditation into her day. Nikki's revenues have doubled in about 18 months – a growth she attributes in no small part to her meditation practice. And, more importantly, she loves her work again; after 20 years in the same line of work, her interest had waned, and she'd felt as though she'd lost her purpose. Nikki takes a few minutes before each big meeting to focus on her breath and get herself present for her clients. This allows her to move on from the last meeting or project she was working on and give her full attention to her client. Since adding short moments for meditation into her day, her referrals have dramatically increased, and she's built a supportive team. I suspect it's because her clients and staff are appreciating her undivided attention, noticing her ability to truly listen to them, and feeling calm in her presence.

## MESSAGE FROM MONEY

*I love it when you think good thoughts about me. I'm thinking good thoughts about you! I'm also sending you messages all the time. Messages that are helpful and guiding. It's hard for you to hear these if you are talking over them. It's hard for me to give you helpful answers to your questions if you are filling your mind with worries and bad thoughts about me and about your abilities to work with me. Please ask me questions and then... shhhh... listen for the answers.*

## Gain Traction Through Action

Thinking about meditating won't get you as far as actually meditating. Here's a quick practice you can use to take a mini-break in your day and calm down any financial inflammation you might be experiencing. Find a quiet setting and set a timer for five minutes. Gently close your eyes or look downward with a soft gaze. Move your attention to your breath; notice your inhales and exhales. When your mind drifts and you notice you are no longer focusing on your breath, gently bring your attention back to the inhales and exhales.

That's it. It's that easy. If you're someone who doesn't feel relaxed when you notice your breath, try noticing sounds, near and far, instead. It's misguided to believe that when you meditate you won't have any thoughts. Our minds are built for thinking! But each time you notice you've lost focus on your breath and bring your attention back to following your inhales and exhales, you're building mental focus. You're telling Margo you're in charge and that it's okay for her to be quiet for a bit.

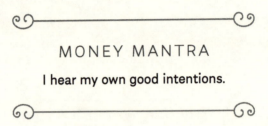

MONEY MANTRA

**I hear my own good intentions.**

## Dude, It's Not My Fault!

It's easy to blame Money for your issues. People often say things like:

"Money changed them."

"Money is such a problem in my life."

"Money messed their kids up."

But Money didn't do any such thing; people did.

Please stop blaming Money for your money problems. Blame can feel appeasing, but can't fix a problem. At first, it feels good to have someone or something to blame. But then you start to feel angry, scared, and frustrated, but not better.

Your relationship with Money – and possibly other

areas of your life – will suffer if you talk badly about it
and blame it for your issues.

**Jessica** In a consultation, Jessica said to me: "I know I
can't be in a good relationship and run a successful
business." I stopped her, pointed out that a great
business and a great romantic relationship are not
mutually exclusive. We talked about this unhelpful
belief. She hadn't seen the possibility of running
her business and being in a loving romantic relationship. Jessica believed it was impossible. She had
blamed Money for past relationship issues she'd
had with partners and was resigned to being single.
With the new belief that she could have both, she
let go of blame. The next time we spoke, Jessica
was in a wonderful new relationship.

Money is a helpful partner who won't cause issues
for you. What causes issues typically is how humans
interact, control, and sometimes ignore Money.
Money doesn't like to be falsely accused and blamed.
Would you?

Instead of blaming Money (or someone else)
for your financial difficulties, what if you explored
Money's gifts? I know this is not easy to do during
financial challenges. But could you be open to the possibility of learning something new or discovering that
this experience could ultimately help someone else?

Many years ago, when our kids were young and I was

early in my career as a financial advisor, Steven and I started to accumulate credit card debt. This happened for a variety of reasons, including having a rental property without a tenant. I was mortified. How could I be a financial advisor with credit card debt?! I blamed my husband. I blamed the economy. As I was crying about all of this to my business coach Phyllis, she listened carefully. Then, in the most tough-love way, she said, "Ellen, I've known you for a long time and I know you know the difference between scarcity thinking and abundance thinking. It sounds like you're coming from a place of scarcity." Damn. She really called me on my stuff. Phyllis was totally right. In that moment, I decided to do whatever I could to change our situation. And I had the glimmer of a thought: *someday I'll be able to tell this story and help someone else.*

> When something challenging or unexpected occurs, it's helpful to consider: this could be a good thing. Then, notice what creativity arises.

I learned from a difficult time. Within a year, we were out of debt. It took a while for me to feel comfortable sharing this story and recognize the lessons from it, but I do remember knowing at the time that growth and gifts were possible, even if I couldn't identify them right in that moment.

When something challenging or unexpected occurs, it's helpful to consider: *this could be a good thing.* Then, notice what creativity arises.

A client you were hoping to secure doesn't hire you. *This could be a good thing.*

Interest rates rise and change the economics of a deal you're working on. *This could be a good thing.*

An unexpected expense comes up. *This could be a good thing.*

This might feel like BS when you first start saying, "This could be a good thing." But what do you have to lose? It might help you to solve your issue or see another opportunity waiting for you.

## MESSAGE FROM MONEY

When you blame me for your problems or think I'm the solution to every challenge, you miss out on the gift. I promise: financial difficulties aren't a punishment. I know that it can be very difficult at times, and it feels stressful when financial uncertainty or major issues arise. I also know that if — even for a moment — you can believe there is learning and growth possible, solutions are easier to find. When you can find ways to quell your fears and quiet your mind, you'll hear the whispers of how to create a different and better reality. Oh, and spending time blaming yourself won't move you ahead, either. Instead, let's support each other and begin to create a new reality.

## Gain Traction Through Action

You'll need a pen, paper, and five minutes of quiet time for this.

Think of a situation in which you blamed Money, another person, or yourself for a financial difficulty or challenge.

Take a moment to notice your breath. Feel the inhales and the exhales.

Set a timer for five minutes and use your pen and paper to complete one or more of the journal prompts below. This is only for you; don't worry about what you are writing, just keep your pen moving.

*Journal Prompts:*
*From this situation, I've learned or am learning...*
*When I think about this situation, I'm grateful for...*
*I am growing because of this situation in these ways...*
*This situation could be a good thing because...*

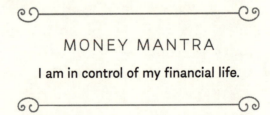

MONEY MANTRA

**I am in control of my financial life.**

## Tap Into Your Money Intuition

Most people in business (and in life) are ignoring one of the most effective ways to meet goals and get ahead with ease.

What am I referring to?

Your inner wisdom – your intuition.

Some believe intuition is some kind of magical, mystical thing that can only be used regularly by a special few.

But intuition is just another sense, another way of knowing, that is accessible to you. Everyone can tap into this. Western culture teaches us to rely more on our thinking mind for information – especially when it comes to money and business. This can be helpful, but if you're solely using your intellect, your reasoning, and your research, you're missing a lot of the information available to you.

> Make inner knowing your not-so-silent business partner.

Not using your intuition in your work is like having an amazing assistant who is eager to help... but you don't trust them to do anything for you. When you *do* give them a job, you keep double checking if they're doing it right.

Make inner knowing your not-so-silent business partner.

I was leading a 'Create Prosperity on Purpose' class, and we talked about how we could best tap into our intuition to support our businesses. One of the participants shared what *not* to do. She said, "Don't cast suspicion on your own feelings."

Building your intuitive abilities is a little like raising confident kids. If you're constantly ignoring them, discounting what they have to say, or shutting their ideas down, they'll have a much harder time speaking up confidently as they get older. This is also true for your intuition. If you ignore and doubt it, you'll stop getting messages, noticing your instincts, and discovering creative ideas which can help guide you.

In preparation for that class, I talked with Money. This is an important way for me to get intuitive hits and creative ideas. What I heard and shared with the group (and then refined based on a conversation with my friend Janice), is that to build your intuitive muscles, you can focus on creating a PACT with Money by using these four ideas:

**Present** – Quiet your chatty mind to notice your own good intentions.

**Aware** – Listen, feel for, and see messages that come your way.

**Curious** – Don't judge what's coming through for you. If you aren't sure what something means, get curious and ask for clarification.

**Trust** – Believing what your gut (your intuition, or whatever you want to call it) is telling you is crucial. A way to prove your trust is to act on it.

I find when I access my internal guidance system, it's like there is a stream of helpful messages all around me. It's like turning up the volume and brightness on your internal GPS to be led in the right direction.

## MESSAGE FROM MONEY

*You are more brilliant, wise, and creative than you give yourself credit for. You are also supported in many ways you cannot see. Energetic forces, collective consciousness, and invisible guides are excited to help you in your journey. When you are quiet enough to hear messages coming your way, aware enough to see signs when they show up for you, and open enough to notice when things feel right, your path becomes clear and your progress more smooth.*

### Gain Traction Through Action

Here are some ways to practice leaning into using your inner knowing:

- Give your intuition a name so that when you ask for help or acknowledge its guidance, you know who you're speaking to. It might be a personal name like Susie, or a more general name like Consciousness. When I'm journaling, I talk to my Divine Partners. When it's about financial concerns for me or people I consult with, I call it *Money*.

- Have regular meetings with your inner knowing via journaling, meditation, walking in nature, or any way that enables you to tap in easily.

- Ask for assistance and don't micromanage. Believe that ideas, insights, inspiration, and solutions will show up.

- If you receive a message that doesn't make total sense to you, ask for another example or sign to clarify or confirm your understanding.

- Ways you can ask for guidance:

    ◦ Write to your intuition when you journal – ask what they want you to know, be, or do.
    ◦ Ask out loud.
    ◦ Ask in your mind.

- Be a great observer; be quiet and present so you can hear, see, and feel messages coming your way.

- Trust! Act on signs you receive.

## MONEY MANTRA

**I trust my inner knowing. I am guided for good.**

## Chapter 6

# Clear

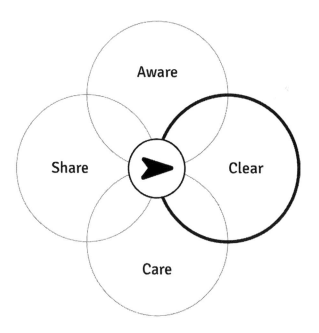

## Your Financial GPS

In my sophomore year in college, I planned a spring-break trip with my friends Debbie, Shari, and Terri. We were headed to Fort Walton Beach, Florida, for four days. A college kid's dream trip including sun, beach, and parties! Debbie and Shari left on a Friday, but Terri and I had mid-term exams and couldn't leave until the next day.

That Saturday morning, we packed up Terri's cool cream-colored Chevy Camaro and set off. Heading out from Tulane University in New Orleans, the drive is relatively easy; you take I-10 East and get off about four hours later at the Fort Walton Beach exit. Terri and I started talking and then talking some more. After a while, I looked at her and said, "Ter, don't you think we should have seen the exit by now?"

This road trip was before there were GPS systems in cars or mobile phones. Back then, if you needed directions, you'd stop at a gas station. That's exactly what we did.

I jumped out of the car, walked inside, and said to the woman behind the counter, "Do you know where the exit is for Fort Walton Beach?" She tilted her head, squinted her eyes, and said, "Do y'all have a map?"

We were in Birmingham, Alabama.

We had driven five hours in the totally wrong direction. Terri and I drove back down five hours and then east a few more hours to finally get where we wanted to go. Our four-hour trip took ten hours. We missed the entire first day of spring break. And we were so embarrassed, we didn't tell Debbie and Shari what happened until we graduated two years later!

I often see similar approaches with goal setting. People have vague ideas of where they want to go and no real plan of how to get there. And then they are frustrated that they're in Birmingham (I'm sure Birmingham is lovely if that indeed is where you want to be; I've never spent much time there!).

The next step in the *Create Prosperity on Purpose Framework* is *Clear*. Having a clear focus is like having a GPS getting you to where you want to go more quickly and easily.

## What Do You Want? Do You Really Really Want?

Being clear about where you want to go is an essential step to getting there. Yet most people don't get specific on what they desire. Others are afraid to commit to their vision because they are worried about how bad it will feel if they don't achieve their goal.

> Money loves it when you are specific about what you desire so it can help you get there more easily. Lack of clarity is like getting in your car and saying to your phone, "Hey Siri, take me there." If I ask my phone this, Siri responds, "Which one?" and gives me options of places with the word take in their name. It wants to help but doesn't know how to.

Money loves it when you are specific about what you desire, so it can help you get there more easily. Lack of clarity is like getting in your car and saying to your phone, "Hey Siri, take me *there*." If I ask my phone this, Siri responds, "Which one?" and gives me options of places with the word *take* in their name. It wants to help but doesn't know how to.

It's common to select an amount of money as a goal. I've seen clients on countless occasions making this mistake: setting a financial number as your goal doesn't work. It's much more effective to make your goal reflect what you ultimately want your money to do for you. We'll talk more about this. For now, I suggest that instead of focusing on having, for example, $50,000 in your bank account, focus instead on what this will *do* for you. Perhaps something like, "My goal is to start and grow my own financially successful coaching business." Having resources in the bank is an important part of the journey there.

People often stop themselves from setting compelling goals because they get stuck thinking about *how* they will achieve them. Focusing on *how* can be limiting at this stage. Trust that when you are clear on where you want to go, the path to get there will be revealed.

### MESSAGE FROM MONEY

I am here on the ride with you. You choose the destination. I'll pick up on your excitement about where we're going. Please make sure you focus on where you want to be instead of on what you don't want to show up for you. It's cool to know what you don't desire, but then move your attention to what you'd like to create. It's more fun that way and easier for me to support you in the process.

## *Gain Traction Through Action*

The late Vedic astrologer, Bill Levacy, once asked me to finish this sentence during a session: "Wouldn't it be cool if…"

I answered, "Wouldn't it be cool if I could be hired to speak at a large conference in Australia? Be flown over, put up in a lovely hotel, and invited to stay on and explore." I'd always wanted to go to Australia because I'd been drawn to the idea of living there for part of the year, and I figured I should visit first! And obviously, it would be cool to have the trip paid for.

I hadn't realized before answering this question how much I wanted to make this happen. But, using the techniques shared in this book, I got there. It didn't happen as quickly as I'd originally thought it should (though I now realize it happened when it was supposed to), but I was hired to speak in Sydney to a large audience, put up in a lovely hotel, and flown over with lots of legroom. It was so cool!

Go ahead and answer this journal prompt for yourself:

*Wouldn't it be cool if…*

To uncover other longer-term goals and desires, create a story of your future life. With the following journal prompt, write as if it's happening right now in the present tense. Include lots of juicy details in your story such as where you are living, what it looks and feels like, who you are hanging out with, the work you are doing, your lifestyle, how you are spending your time, and how you are positively impacting others. Don't rush this process. Grab a cup of tea or your favorite beverage, and settle in with your pen and paper to answer the following prompt.

> *Date your journal five years from today.*
> *Imagine you're being interviewed by someone who is very interested in your life. They ask, "Tell me about yourself and your life?"*

## MONEY MANTRA

**I am clear, confident, and on my path to prosperity.**

## From Goal Setting to Goal Getting

Goals can be double-edged swords. They feel exciting and motivating as you set them, but discouraging when they aren't achieved.

At the end of the first 10 years of my financial advisory business, I was to meet with my coach, Phyllis, to look at the plan for the next year. I felt both excited and discouraged.

I love planning, envisioning, and strategizing about where I want to go. That part of the plan was super fun. But, when I looked back on the previous year, I felt discouraged as I hadn't hit the goals I'd set at the beginning of the year. It suddenly occurred to me that I'd been repeating to myself, "I never reach my business goals." And this unhelpful belief unintentionally supported me in never reaching my business goals!

I stopped repeating this unhelpful belief, and instead focused on what I had achieved during the year. At the end of each year, I now make a list of what went well, and I also create a highlight reel with pictures I've taken during the year to remind myself of all the awesome things that happened.

These new practices help, but the biggest changes in my business success happened when I created my Goal Getting Process.

## The Goal-Getting Process

By following the Goal-Getting Process steps, I was able to grow my business revenues by 39 percent within one year and break through a plateau I'd been stuck at for a while. This different approach to goals has also brought big results to clients who've tried it.

There are four steps in the Goal-Getting Process:

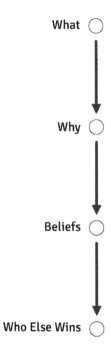

For each goal you set, explore:

**What** do you specifically desire? Remember, being clear about where you want to go is an essential step to getting there.

**Why** is this important to you? If you say, "I want to earn $500,000" – why? Is it to provide financial security for your family? Send your kids to college? Donate more money to charity? Take a trip to Costa Rica? Perhaps these are the actual goals. For me (and most of my clients), a specific amount of money isn't usually the goal; the goal is what that money could do for you. The money is a way to measure your progress.

What **beliefs** do you have about achieving this goal? Understanding your beliefs about what is possible and what you can make happen is crucial. It's hard to get where you want to go if you are constantly telling yourself that it will never happen.

I've found it important to have coaches and friends in my life who can hold bigger visions for my future than I can sometimes hold for myself. When I started my career as a financial advisor, my dad said to me, "Honey, you'll eventually open your own firm." I remember thinking, "No, I don't see that for me." His confidence and small comment planted a seed that grew in my consciousness and eventually helped me to see myself as a business owner.

Paying attention to **who else wins** is a secret weapon in goal achievement, yet it's most often ignored. Explore who else is served by you achieving each of your goals. Focusing outside of yourself and instead on serving others is incredibly motivating.

When I was a financial advisor, I grew my business during a recession by focusing on others. I moved from only thinking about growing my business to focusing on how people needed me and my advice more than ever. They were scared. I put all my attention on easing their suffering around money. Of course, I still had my goals playing in the background, but I energetically led with being of service to them. My clients felt this. The prospects I met with were swayed to work with me not by my credentials, but by my compassion.

Each of your goals can have a component that helps others, even if it's not obvious at first. For example, if you have a goal to run a marathon, it might seem at first that this only serves you. But wouldn't your commitment also inspire others? Perhaps you could also run for a charity as well to raise money for a good cause.

The last marathon I ran, I raised money for the American Cancer Society. My sister-in-law had ovarian cancer, and I ran with her name on my shirt. A client of mine happened to be volunteering as a photographer for the race and caught a picture of me with Andrea's name on my back. I had no idea how this would touch Andrea. She had been an athlete before her illness and said to me before she passed away, "Ellen, I had always wanted to run a marathon, and I know I never will now. I felt like I was running with you. Thank you."

Who will you be helping, inspiring, or contributing to when you reach your goal?

## MESSAGE FROM MONEY

*What if you knew that I was 100 percent behind you achieving your goals? I love to show up for people when they are doing their best work, making a difference for others, and creating a beautiful life. Yes, I know you may think that sometimes in the past, that wasn't the case. I was just helping you learn and get ready for your big thing. I love it when you focus on positively impacting others, and please remember you will win as well. I see your greatness. I've got your back. Trust in this.*

### Gain Traction Through Action

Explore your discoveries from journaling about your future vision and identify three high-priority goals. For each goal, consider the following.

**What**: Write your goal in the present tense. Make sure to note what you want as opposed to what you don't want. For example, "I easily attract, hire, and retain a wonderful assistant" is more effective than "I want to hire a great assistant," or "I stop hiring the wrong people for the job."

**Why**: Ask yourself why you want this goal. Then ask yourself why you want *that*. Understanding your motivation for your goals will help you to determine if they are actually goals you desire. For example,

"I grow my income by 20 percent this year."

Why?

"To have more money to move into a new home."

Why?

"So that my kids can grow up in a better school district."

It may take a few layers of "Why?" to get to your true motivators. Clarity on your *why* will open up other doors to finding out *how* to accomplish your goal.

**Beliefs**: Journal about your perceived ability to achieve your goal. Here's a suggested prompt:

*What I believe about my abilities to achieve this goal...*

Take your time with this. Be honest with yourself. No one else needs to see this.

After you've completed this, note next to each belief if it is helpful or unhelpful. Cross the unhelpful beliefs out; they are just beliefs and not reality (although they may feel true). How could you replace them with something more supportive? What can you write that you can believe (or work toward believing)? For example, instead of saying: "I suck at marketing," what if you said: "I'm learning new ways to expand my network," or, "Every day, I'm getting better at sharing about my work," or, "I'm great at learning from my mistakes and making changes going forward."

MONEY MANTRA

I easily achieve my goals.

## Dress Rehearsal for Success

As previously mentioned, I've always loved shows, movies, and books that involve a character with magical abilities. As a little girl, I used to imagine I could waive a wand, rub a lamp, or say a secret phrase to make things happen. Captivated by Tabitha Stephens,

Harry Potter, Mary Poppins, and Aladdin, I was inspired to mysteriously conjure what I wished for.

When I started to learn more about the power of our minds, I realized that we have many seemingly magical abilities to turn our visions into realities.

I love manifesting goals through visualization, using my mind's eye to imagine what I want to happen. It's like a dress rehearsal for your goals.

I first learned the power of visualization when I was in high school. I was always in the highest math classes but struggled to perform well on tests. As a result, I believed I was bad at math. Coming from a family where academic success was highly valued, my parents tried to support me and find tutors to help me. In my senior year, I worked with a tutor who said to me: "Ellen, you're great at understanding the concepts, what you need is help taking tests." On the night before and the morning of my exam, he instructed me to picture myself sitting down at my desk with my pencil sharpened, feeling calm. Then seeing the teacher placing the exam in front of me. I imagined knowing all of the answers, writing them down correctly, and finishing the test with plenty of time to spare. Then I pictured the teacher handing us back our tests and seeing a big red A on top of mine.

I did just that. And I got an A. I've used this technique ever since for everything from important sales conversations to speaking events and so much more.

If you'd told me before I learned this process that

I would go on to become an economics major and get an advanced degree with a focus on accounting, I never would have believed you. I also never would have imagined I'd go on to teach this process to people around the world.

As journalist and author William Zinsser is quoted as saying: "Thought is action in rehearsal!"

Early in my financial advisor career, I had an appointment with a prospective client, a corporate executive. Sitting in the waiting room on the thirtieth floor of an office building in downtown Chicago, I was starting to feel nervous. I was 29 years old; he was about 40. I had only been in business for a couple of years; he was the vice president of a global company. Instead of focusing on my lack of experience and feeling intimidated by his corporate position, I imagined how I wanted the meeting to go. I pictured us having a great conversation in which I answered his questions with confidence and ease. I imagined him hiring me and us having a wonderful working relationship. This process not only helped me to be calm and present during our meeting, but eventually led to him and his wife working with me until I left my business almost 26 years later.

I've seen this process work over and over for the people I advise. Angela starts each day by visualizing exactly how she wants her meetings to flow. Before each appointment, she takes five minutes to calm her mind and envision the ideal outcomes. She describes this as one of the reasons her revenues have grown so substantially and her referrals have increased over the last year.

Most people can see pictures in their mind. There is a small percentage of people who have aphantasia, the inability to visualize. After a presentation on using our minds as a tool for success, which I gave to an audience of about 500 people in financial services, a man approached me and said he indeed had aphantasia; he was unable to picture images in his mind. Although this had been true his whole life, he'd only just learned that he saw the world differently from others.

If you are someone on the aphantasia spectrum, this prosperity practice of mental rehearsal might not be for you. Instead, you can practice the facial expressions you'd make when you experience achieving your goal and feel in your body what you'll feel. Will you smile, laugh, feel joy or peace? You could imagine you've just been given the outcome you desire, and respond aloud. Or, roleplay with a friend how you would like an ideal conversation to go. These exercises will have a similar impact as visualization exercises because they too act as mental rehearsals.

## Creating A Prosperity Picture

Creating a prosperity picture is a fun way to envision your future that works for most people. I've seen this be effective in my consulting with one of the wealthiest men in Europe and his teenage son, as well as with high school and university students in rural Ghana. It's not about how much money you have, it's about creating a vision for your future.

A prosperity picture is like a vision board; it's a place where you can gather images that represent goals and use this collection to inspire you moving forward. A prosperity picture, however, takes this concept further by organizing images based upon time and money.

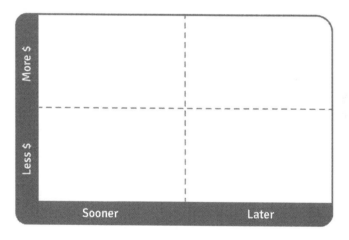

The bottom half of your board is for images relating to goals that require little-to-no money, and the top half is for ones that require more financial resources. The left side of your board is for goals you'd like to achieve sooner (in five years or less), and the right side is for goals you'd like to see happen further down the road.

For example, you might put an image of someone

meditating in the lower left part of your frame, representing you starting or continuing a meditation practice. You want to do this now, and it won't require money. In the upper right part of your prosperity picture, you might have an image of an airplane, reflecting your desire to take an extended trip to Southeast Asia in the future.

I mentioned earlier about my goal to be hired to speak in Australia. I had an image of Australia on my prosperity picture for quite a while. It was on the right side of the frame, somewhere in between more money and less money. The goal was to be flown over and paid to speak there, but I also imagined traveling while I was there. The image is still there but now represents wanting to spend my winters there.

You can download images to help you get started on your prosperity picture at www.messagesfrommoney. com/extras:

Once your prosperity picture is complete, hang it where you will see it on a regular basis. Mine is in my office, above my desk. I also have a picture of it on my phone as the background wallpaper.

Let me be clear on the magic part of the prosperity picture process. It's not merely putting images on a board as a mystical process that helps you realize your goals. It's that these images are in front of you on a regular basis which helps you pay attention to opportunities, resources, and people that can help you move your goals forward. It's rare that putting an image in front of you will be enough to have it show up in your life. Action is crucial. Is this a limiting belief on my part? Perhaps, but I don't think you'll regret taking steps to move your goals ahead more quickly.

If you're interested in learning more about this tool, you'll find it covered in more detail in my book, *'Picture Your Prosperity: Smart Money Moves to Turn Your Vision into Reality.'*

## MESSAGE FROM MONEY

When you picture your goals, I am more able to help you. I love witnessing how excited and clear you are about what you desire. I love being your prosperity partner. Have fun with this process! Be childlike in using the power of your imagination. Remember to see as many details as possible, feel how you'll feel as your goal materializes and how others will feel as well. We can do great things together — let's imagine this being so.

## Gain Traction Through Action

On one of my trips to Ghana, I spoke with Mustapha, a scholarship recipient in the community. As we were walking through the village, he said to me, "Auntie Ellen, is it okay that I daydream?" I responded,

"Everyone daydreams; what do you mean?" We walked on and he explained, "Well, when I was a little boy, I used to picture in my mind going to university, and I'd feel so excited about learning and being there, even though I didn't know anyone who even went to high school, let alone studied beyond that."

Mustapha was the first child from his neighborhood to go to high school. At that time, there was no way for most to come up with the school fees. But he kept picturing his education. By the time he reached high school age, The Ghana Scholarship Fund had started, and he was one of the first recipients.

I named the following *Deliberate Daydream Process* for Mustapha.

Here's the five-step Deliberate Daydream Process to visualize your goals and turn them into reality.

**Step 1 – Think:** Pick your goal. It can be a short- or long-term goal. I suggest you start with something smaller that you want to see happen within the next week. Perhaps a call or a meeting that you want a specific outcome from. If your goal doesn't have a location, give it one like a movie set.

**Step 2 – See:** Picture your goal in your mind's eye. Imagine your goal playing out exactly like you'd love to see it as if it's happening right now.

Notice in detail:

Where are you?

What do you see?

What does the air feel like?

Are there aromas you smell?

Are there sounds you hear?

Are there other people there? If so, who? What are they saying to you and what are you saying to them?

**Step 3 – Feel:** What will you feel as your goal is happening? Happy? Excited? Calm? Go ahead and feel that feeling. Where in your body are you feeling it? Don't skip this step; it's the secret sauce of effectiveness in the process.

**Step 4 – Declare:** What declarative statement about your goal could you create? When I ran in the Chicago Marathon, my statement was: "I train for, run in, and recover from the Chicago Marathon with joy, ease, comradery, and good health." Each marathon I ran in, I added something else to this statement. The goal in my first marathon was simply to finish it. It sucked. It hurt and was boring to train and run in. I added *joy, ease,* and *comradery* after that. Then I realized I needed to add *recover from* and *in good health* after I passed a kidney stone four days after one race. During a training run, I was telling my running group friend Todd about my declarative phrase and stopped right in the middle of a sentence. I realized that our pace group leader's name was Joy! When I was imagining running with joy, this isn't what I was expecting! It was a great reminder that I need to be careful what I declare. Things may show up differently than you imagine.

**Step 5 – Act:** At the end of your visualization, think about what your next step is. Is there someone you could reach out to? Research you need to do? A creative idea you want to write about? Quite often, inspired actions become clear. Make sure you jot down ideas, action steps, and inspired thoughts that arise. It's easy to forget these.

This process only takes a few minutes. I suggest you practice it often. After meditation, when you first wake up in the morning, and before you fall asleep at night are great times. It's also very helpful right before a big meeting, call, or speaking engagement.

If you'd like to spend a bit more time on this, you can access a guided visualization which walks you through this process at www.messagesfrommoney. com/extras:

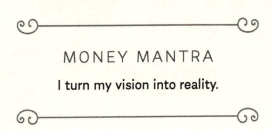

MONEY MANTRA

**I turn my vision into reality.**

## What's Your Prosperity Prompt?

Remember pocket angels? The small coin-like trinkets with an angel on the front? I loved them; they're what started me down the path of collecting talismans. I have a lot of stones, coins, crystals, and trinkets. A lot. So many, I told our kids that when I die, they can give them as gifts to people who show up for the funeral and at the house.

They make me smile when I see them, I feel good when I hold them, and I love to gift them to people. When I speak to groups in person, I often bring glass stones for the audience as a prosperity prompt. I've even embedded a few glass stones in the walkway to my office to remind me every time I walk into our building that prosperity is all around.

In addition to having a prosperity picture where you can see your future vision, it's helpful to keep other symbols around that remind you of the abundance you're surrounded by.

### MESSAGE FROM MONEY

*Abundance surrounds you all the time. Walk into nature and you'll see what I mean. In the spring, there is an abundance of flowers, and birds singing. Whether you can see them or not, you know we are surrounded by an abundance of stars. There is also an abundance of me. There is more than enough of me to go around.*

*Yes, I know sometimes it feels like there is not enough of me but believe me, I'm there. And, yes, you do deserve me! If it's hard to see how this is so, imagine, as with the stars; I'm there. When you can focus on the ways that I am showing up for you, and lean into your thankfulness, you'll see more of me. It's like getting away from the city lights on a clear night — all of a sudden, the stars appear!*

## Gain Traction Through Action

Create your own prosperity prompts. What are ways you can keep reminders of abundance in front of you? Make sure they make you feel good when you see them. Here are some suggestions:

- Photos of beautiful places
- Trinkets and tokens with inspirational words and images
- Water features such as fountains
- Cultural symbols of prosperity and good fortune, such as horseshoes, four-leaf clovers, elephants, pigs, etc.
- Fresh flowers
- Crystal hearts, jewelry, and stones (green jade, tiger eye, malachite, citrine, pyrite, green aventurine, and clear quartz are believed to attract

and enhance prosperity) – go for what you are attracted to!

- Colors that represent wealth and prosperity to *you*. For example, purple, gold, white, green and red. For me it's deep blues and purples. My father always said, "Ell, don't sign your name in red; it means debt." So that wouldn't be a color I would choose. But perhaps it's a good-luck one for you, like it is in some East Asian cultures.

- And, of course, your prosperity picture.

## Chapter 7

# Care

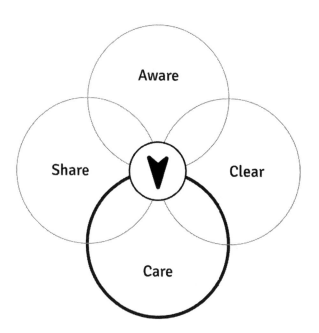

## It Takes More than Love

If you're a parent, you know it takes more than just love to raise children. Yes, love is crucial, but you also must be involved and care for them. Having a child-care provider (even a great one) making all of the decisions about your kids while you just show up to hug them once in a while... won't work out well.

It's the same for your money. Money wants you to care about it, know what's going on with it, and make sure it's healthy and growing.

This doesn't mean you can't delegate some of the management of your finances to a trusted advisor or partner, but it's crucial you know what's happening with it, understand how it's working in your life, and make sure it's being cared for responsibly.

Money lives in both the material world and the ethereal world. Most of us need Money to function well in the material world. Caring for the well-being of your money means spending and saving consciously, growing your money wisely, protecting what you have, making sure others dependent on you are financially cared for, and having sources of money flowing to you. The ethereal components of money are the unseen parts, including your relationship with Money, your inclination to use your money as a force for good, the power of your mind to help create what you desire, and your generosity.

If someone only focuses on the material parts of

managing their money, they may end up with a lot of it, but they're likely to have no contentment and fight with their partner about money or use it to control others. On the other hand, if you sit on your meditation pillow chanting and never take action to take care of your personal finances, that typically doesn't work either.

Focusing your attention on both the material and ethereal is the path to true prosperity.

## Don't Be a Stalker or a Sleepwalker with Your Money

Clearly, avoiding looking at your money and investments can lead to problems over time. But on the other end of the attention/avoidance scale, paying *too* much attention can lead to issues as well.

**Michelle** One of my friends, Michelle, shared with me that her husband, Joe, was obsessed with looking at their investments and watching the financial news. When I say obsessed, I mean checking the values of his investments hourly during the day. Like a stalker, Joe tracked every move his money made. When the markets were rocky, it would affect his mood and he'd become depressed and angry. Michelle is a financial advisor. She'd created a sound plan for their financial future. Joe's fixed

attention on their investments was not only hurt-
ing his mental health and their relationship, but it
could also impact their financial health.

Paying too much attention can also show up in
micromanaging spending and saving. Does it make
sense to know where your money is going? Sure! We'll
talk about this more. But does it make sense to focus
on every single penny spent? Let me ask you this: if
your partner is scrutinizing every purchase – how does
that make you feel? My guess is that it feels restrictive,
like you're going against the current.

If you are someone who needs to focus more on
saving, this might be a shock to you, but some people
*over*-save. They are so worried about not having
enough down the road, they have trouble enjoying
their money currently. Joan was an over-saver. Her
parents grew up during the Great Depression and
felt terrified of being without money. Joan inherited
this fear-based approach to her money. The helpful
part of this was that Joan saved a lot of money. This
gave her flexibility when she was laid off from her job
before she found her next opportunity. The unhelpful impact was that she lived in constant worry about
her finances. Her financial advisor ran projections for
her, and she was on track with cushions for her retirement goals. Yet she had high money anxiety. Joan lived
in self-impoverishment.

If you avoid dealing with your money and you

sleepwalk through your financial life, perhaps paying too much attention, carefully tracking all of your spending, and over-saving feel like problems you'd like to have. Depending on your favorite flavor of money-worry, you might be an over-saver and an avoider. Money doesn't like to be controlled too much; it also doesn't like to be ignored, wasted, or left to wither away.

Delegating the management of your money to another person might be a healthier alternative to burying your head in the sand and paying no attention, but you must still know what is happening. Why is turning over total control of your finances unwise if you have a trusted advisor or family member managing your money? It could be an issue for several reasons. The person who is managing the money might get sick, die, or leave you. Or they might not be as trustworthy as you think.

When I was a financial advisor, I worked with a woman who lost her husband to suicide. Clearly shocked, with two small kids, she had absolutely no knowledge of their family finances. Not only was she dealing with a tragedy, she also had to put the financial pieces of their life together. Fortunately, he left their family in solid financial shape, and she had a trusted friend who came with her to our meetings to help ease her into her new role as the financial caretaker.

I've also seen two situations where people turned their business finances over to people they believed were *trusted* partners. They did this despite having a deep understanding of how money works (one was even a financial advisor). They wanted to be uninvolved in the bookkeeping parts of their businesses and focus their attention on business growth. In both situations, their partners stole money from the business – lots of it.

I've had several clients whose parents have stolen money from them. This happened when they were minors and weren't in a position to be more involved. Sometimes, financial trauma is out of your control. When I talk to Money about this, I learn that these difficult situations build self-reliance muscles; they teach us about trust and, over time, healthy growth. This is not to say that it's easy.

Trust with Money is important. Most people are honest with Money. But some are not. Knowing what's happening with your finances is crucial.

Financial well-being involves a balance of care and attention with joy and involvement.

## MESSAGE FROM MONEY

*Please spend time with me. I love to be with you, and I know deep down you appreciate me. I want you to know me, to care for me, and to work with me. I don't require a huge amount of your attention, just enough. How do you know if your balance is right with me? Notice how much time you focus on me. Are we good?*

Here's the thing. I show up for people when I know they want me around. And one way I know this is when there is caring energy directed at me. Notice I said caring energy, not desperate, controlling, or abusive energy. Who would want to be around that?!

## Gain Traction Through Action

If you haven't yet assessed where you fall on the Money MO chart in Chapter Two, go ahead and do that now.

**If you lean toward money-stalking:**

- **Go on a financial news fast for one week.** Does just thinking about that give you a pit in your stomach? That pit indicates how good this step would be for you. Unless you're actively trading your investments daily (which may be a problem as well), one week without financial media will not hurt you. As a financial advisor, I did not watch the financial news daily. With a long-term plan in place, this kind of monitoring is unnecessary.

- **Spend money on someone else.** We'll talk more in the next chapter about sharing, but for now, let's loosen your grip on money a bit. Go buy a gift for someone for no reason. Don't be cheap.

Or make a charitable donation to a cause you really believe in. If you live in a city with people who are unhoused, perhaps you could buy a meal for someone you see who is asking for money on the street.

- **Support someone in your life to pay more attention to money.** If you are high on attention, you might also be high on control. Who in your life is affected by you doing everything for them? A child? A partner? A parent? If something happens to you, will this other person know how to pick up the pieces? If your answer to this question is: "They can just call _____ (fill in the blank with a trusted friend or advisor), and they'll take over," this is hindering your loved one in their relationship with Money. Your challenge might be supporting them without judgment. I've heard over and over: "They don't want to be involved." Really? Or is it that you haven't found the right way to communicate with them? Get an advisor or therapist involved if you need help. When I was a financial advisor, I had several clients who didn't really need my technical knowledge; they brought me in so that their less involved spouse could know what was going on and feel comfortable asking questions to learn more.

If you're more of a sleepwalker with Money:

- **Schedule a meeting with your money.** Whether you do this on your own, with your financial advisor, or with your partner, at least once a year, schedule time to understand the following:
    - What you own and owe. This is a review of your assets and liabilities.
    - What you have spent and where (more on this in the next section).
    - How much you've saved over the last 12 months.
    - Are your investments aligned with your goals and risk comfort level?
    - What happens if there is an unexpected death, disability, or job loss? Do you have the right types of insurance in place and your estate plan updated? Do you know where your important documents are and how to access them?

If you want more information on these areas, you might want to read *Picture Your Prosperity: Smart Money Moves to Turn Your Vision into Reality*.

- **Get to know Money better.** Sometimes, people avoid dealing with their money because it feels complicated. Or perhaps they feel a

little embarrassed that they don't understand
some financial concepts or the details about
their situation.

Here are three suggestions to up your financial
knowledge:

- Work with a good financial advisor or financial coach who creates a judgment-free zone.
  They wouldn't have a business if everyone
  was a personal-finance expert. It's their
  job to help their clients understand money
  better. If you feel like there isn't a safe space
  to share and learn with your advisor, find a
  different one. Many of the financial advisors
  I know have educational programs for their
  clients for just this purpose.

- If you hear a financial term you don't know,
  do a quick search online. If you've read a
  book on an e-reader, you know that you can
  highlight a word and it will give you a definition. It's a great tool for expanding your
  vocabulary. It might not be that seamless
  with financial terms, but it is still quick.

- Watch a few minutes of the financial news a
  few times a week. I sometimes recommend
  avoiding the financial news if it makes someone anxious or they spend too much time
  focusing on the markets, but it might be just
  what you need to start learning the language.

You don't have to be fluent in financial speak, but conversational is helpful.

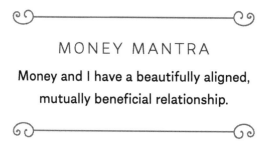

## MONEY MANTRA

**Money and I have a beautifully aligned, mutually beneficial relationship.**

## Get Intimate with Your Money

We've talked a lot about your internal relationship with Money. How your thoughts and beliefs about Money impact your results. It is also important that you understand the external details about your money and manage it well.

When I was a financial advisor, we helped to ensure that our clients' finances were set up to help them achieve their goals. There was a lot that went into creating a financial plan, and there are certain areas that are fundamental to driving success.

Over the years, I saw that one of the biggest success levers is a focus on saving. Yes, some folk are wildly wealthy based upon selling businesses, making investments that hit it big, receiving an inheritance, or winning the lottery, but not many. For most people, it's the less sexy work of being a consistent saver that got them to their financial goals.

Many people in financial services might not agree with me on this, but I believe that being a great saver is more important than being a savvy investor. Yes, of course you want your money working for you. But I've seen lots of people have secure retirements, send their kids to good schools, and enjoy their lifestyles without a big focus on their investments. To me, at a very practical level, saving well and making good money decisions will get you farther than a focus on eking out an extra two percent return. If you can do both – strong saving *and* savvy investing – good for you.

For most people, it takes eating good food and exercising regularly to maintain a healthy weight. If you eat lots of fast food and lie on your couch streaming shows, you'll likely deal with the physical effects. Similarly, if you

> If you want to have financial well-being, spend consciously and save deliberately for maximum impact.

have tons of credit card debt and little or no savings from unconscious spending, you won't likely reach your goals, and will experience lots of stress.

I know this is easier said than done (just as with losing weight). This is why the *Aware, Clear, Care,* and *Share* sections of the *Prosperity on Purpose Framework* are so important. The practices in these sections help to build positive beliefs and habits to support you in adjusting how you take care of your money on a practical level.

If you want to have financial well-being, spend consciously and save deliberately for maximum impact.

For many people at certain points in life, it isn't possible to save. And I've also witnessed many people with limited financial resources be very good at spending less than they earn.

Most of the strategies in this book will help you do the internal work to be a better saver. Here I want to talk about the practical steps.

Many financial advisors won't agree with me on this one either: I don't like budgets. Why? I've rarely seen them work. They feel restrictive – like being on a diet.

> I don't like budgets. Why? I've rarely seen them work. They feel restrictive – like being on a diet. That doesn't mean I don't think it's smart to know where you're spending your money. Most people have no idea what they spend and where it goes. You absolutely should know where and how you're spending money. Money doesn't like to be wasted. But what if, instead of a budget, you established a values-based spending plan? Doesn't a plan for spending sound more fun? It will also be more effective.

That doesn't mean I don't think it's smart to know where you're spending your money. Most people have no idea what they spend and where it goes. You absolutely should know where and how you're spending money. Money doesn't like to be wasted.

But what if, instead of a budget, you established a values-based spending plan? Doesn't a plan for spending sound more fun? It will also be more effective.

> Instead of a budget, establish a prioritized spending strategy.

Instead of a budget, establish a prioritized spending strategy.

How do you do this? Either using an app, cash-flow tracking software, spreadsheet, or just pen and paper, list out what you've spent in the last 12 months and where it went. It's helpful to track this in detail so you can assess whether your spending has been funneled into areas you value.

Next, review the areas you've spent your money on and decide if they are A, B, or C priorities. A-listers relate to things they really love and value. B-spending categories are important, but you would cut them back or out if you had to. Items that are Cs are either nice-to-haves or places you spend money but really don't care about.

I've often seen people go through this exercise and realize areas that initially seemed important to them really weren't. For example, Julia realized that her home was no longer something she really valued. Her kids were grown and out of the house, it was filled with belongings she didn't care about, and she still had a mortgage and all the other expenses that came along with her home. Looking at her expenses through a values-based lens helped her realize that it was time to move. Once she'd sold her house and bought a smaller home, she was able to leave a job she hated and find more meaningful work.

Creating a values-based spending plan is a big project if you aren't currently tracking your spending. I promise: if you create your spending plan, you'll be glad you did. Armed with this information, you'll be able to make decisions, create a long-term financial strategy, and build a better relationship with your money.

## MESSAGE FROM MONEY

*I want us to be tight. I want to better understand what you care about, and I want you to better understand how I work in your life. You may think I'm boring. You may think I'm hard to understand. You may think dealing with me is someone else's job. But none of this is true. If you think it's fun to have me around, please don't treat me poorly. I want more than a casual relationship with you. Let's build a beautiful future together. To make this happen more easily, please show me you care about me. Spending with care and saving with love are great starts.*

## Gain Traction Through Action

Each of us has at least one area of our money we know needs attention; something that has been periodically playing in the background as a nagging thought. It might sound like:

"Oh! I really need to pay that bill!"

"I know I need to increase my retirement contributions but it's such a pain and I don't have time."

> The projects you're avoiding, even if you aren't consciously thinking about them, are taking energy away from more creative tasks. Having a task that needs your attention is like having a pebble in your shoe. Once you take care of it, you can move ahead more easily.

"I'm supposed to get back to Trevor about that insurance he talked to us about. It feels so complicated I don't have the bandwidth for that right now."

"I've been meaning to…"

Our daughter Amy has an investment account that she couldn't access online as there was an error with the social security number listed. Without online access, it's difficult to make changes to her account. It's held at a giant financial services company where it's hard to get a real person on the phone. When she finally did speak with someone, they said she needed to complete a form and email it back.

Amy doesn't have a printer. This is a pain for her to do. She still hasn't fixed her account.

The projects you're avoiding, even if you aren't consciously thinking about them, are taking energy away from more creative tasks. Having a task that needs your attention is like having a pebble in your shoe. Once you take care of it, you can move ahead more easily.

**What are you putting off?** Take some time and make a list. You'll recognize the tasks that will make you feel better once you've handled them. Here are some I've seen free up attention for people once cleaned up:

- Consolidating bank accounts
- Updating beneficiaries on your accounts
- Organizing files
- Getting referrals and meeting with professionals who can help (financial advisors, accountants, attorneys, etc.)
- Review your finances with your partner to make sure you're on the same page and that both know what's going on
- Set up online access to your investment accounts
- Organize your passwords so you and your partner can easily find them.

Once you begin to take action and gain momentum, you'll find other elements of caring for your money come more easily. Here are some areas that will have a big impact and help to move your financial plan ahead:

- **Where's the cash dashing to?** Creating a prioritized spending plan, as described above, will help you spend more consciously and enable you to be present with where you are currently spending. Why should you care about this? It's not to beat yourself up, or to feel guilty about your daily trip to your favorite coffeehouse. It's to wake up to the way money flows through your life and to have the information needed to create a plan for getting to your goals.

- **Set your savings plan on automatic pilot.** I recently rewatched 'Airplane!' which holds up shockingly well for a movie that came out in 1980. The scenes with the blow-up auto-pilot come to mind when I think about setting up savings to happen on a regular basis. As an advisor, I never had a client say to me that they wished they *hadn't* saved for their future. Putting away money now for a future goal such as a big trip, starting a business, or retirement, gives you options and flexibility. It's much easier to make this happen when you set up your savings to initiate automatically. Having money taken from your paycheck or checking account each month makes the process less painful. You could even start with a small amount and up it over time; it will add up.

- **Pay off that credit card.** It's hard to get ahead financially if you have credit card debt. Chances are, you are paying a high interest rate on the outstanding balances. Growing your financial stability while you have this type of debt is like trying to fill a bathtub with the drain open. Credit card debt can also be a significant cause of stress and have a negative impact on your health. Your debt may be there due to unexpected medical expenses, a job loss, or overspending. If you need help in this area, find a reputable credit counselling service that can work with you to consolidate your debt and come up with a payment plan.

- **What's your safety net?** If something happens to you, will your family be okay financially? If you become disabled or die, will the bills get paid, and will your loved ones be able to stay where they're living, at least for a while? Equally, if you're dependent on someone else's income or assets and something happens to them, will you be okay? If not, life, disability, or long-term care insurance might be good solutions. If you're not sure, review what you have. If you don't understand what you have, seek help from a professional.

- **The love letter to your family after you're gone.** If there's one area I've seen people procrastinate on, it's getting their will, trust, and powers of attorney completed. I've even been the person dragging their feet on getting it done! But without a good plan in place, you're leaving your family at risk and setting them up to be frustrated with you when you're gone. What do you want to happen to your assets and your belongings when you die? Who will take care of your kids if something happens to you? How do you want to be cared for at the end of your life and who do you want to make these decisions if you are unable to yourself? This is grown-up stuff that needs to be handled. Don't wait for your next vacation to get it done (I'm not sure why, but a big trip sometimes is a motivator for people to finally do their estate plan). Please just do this.

- **Are you growing your money in ways that make sense for you?** Once you've saved your money, make sure it's working for you. It's a good idea to have an amount set aside as a cushion for unexpected opportunities or bumps in the road. The amount varies by your situation, but between 3 and 12 months of living expenses is a good target. This is money you'll want to be able to access if you need it without penalties or the risk that it will be worth less than what you put into the accounts. Savings or money market accounts might be an option for you. Money invested for the longer term can be invested with more growth potential. With more growth comes more risk that the value can go *down*. It's important to understand what you are investing in and make sure that you can stomach any volatility you may experience in exchange for a bigger potential return.

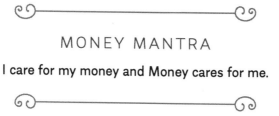

MONEY MANTRA

I care for my money and Money cares for me.

## You Are Great with Money!

In the movie 'The Help,' the maid Aibileen, played by Viola Davis, says to the little girl Mae (whom she cares for), "You is kind. You is smart. You is important." Mae was often berated by her mother. When it comes to talking about Money, there's lots of critical, shaming, finger-wagging energy. Most people focus on what they aren't doing well with money instead of their financial strengths. I've never heard Money tell anyone, "You suck at finances." Instead, the messages are much more like Aibileen's; they sound like, "You are smart. You are creative. You are doing great."

I was networking once with a life coach, Susan, and she said to me, "If one more person tells me to organize my financial records, I'll go crazy. I am *never* going to do this!" I realized in that moment that most financial advice is given to *everyone* regardless of their strengths or approach. Susan could reach all of her goals and never organize her financial records.

There are many ways to reach your long-term goals; we don't all need to get there the same way. Yet often, financial guidance is given as if there's only one path. This would be like telling someone, "If you want to be healthy and live a long life, you must each kale three times a week, do yoga for 60 minutes four times a week, and walk 10,000 steps each and every day." This is not to entirely discredit this advice; I'm sure eating kale, doing yoga, and walking are (usually) good for your health, just like consolidating your bank accounts, organizing your files, and meeting with professionals will likely increase your financial well-being. But there is no one-size-fits-all approach to health nor money.

Everyone has something they are great at when it comes to money. A focus on your strengths instead of your weaknesses can move you along more quickly. And yes, you may need to delegate tasks that you are less than excellent at completing yourself. Having a clear understanding about what you are good at will help you decide areas you need to delegate or get support on from an advisor or trusted friend.

People think that they need to be detail-oriented,

fascinated with investments, and great at math to be good with money. If that were the case, every math teacher and engineer would be financially set and content with their money. There are many other traits and skills that are relevant to caring for money.

When I began my career as a financial advisor, I was convinced that I had to love dealing with the minutia of people's financial lives, be able to get lost in the spreadsheets, and find joy in investment analytics. After a while, I came to know that I could hire people who were skilled at these things and instead focus on my strengths of big-picture thinking, a calm approach, and easily finding solutions for my clients.

I remember a woman I helped after her divorce. She told me, "I'm terrible with money." She didn't find joy in tracking her expenses, balancing her bank accounts, and reading up on financial trends. She may have also heard from her ex, a teacher, or a parent that she wasn't good with money, and she believed them. This woman negotiated the best divorce settlement I'd ever seen. She was also great at spending deliberately and finding deals to help her save money. Far from terrible in my eyes.

Where are your strengths when it comes to money? Perhaps you excel at one of the following:

**Mindset** – You think optimistically and prosperously. Do you have helpful beliefs such as, "There's always gotta be a way" or, "Things always work out for me"? This abundance mindset is an important part of making calm decisions and finding opportunities for growth.

**Organization** – You know the details of your finances. Not only is this helpful for you, but also for others involved in your financial life. People who are very organized tend to notice errors in their accounts and resolve them quicker. They also tend to act on opportunities more quickly as they know what they have. If you're working with an advisor, they will do better work if you are able to give them more detailed information.

**Planning** – You are good at mapping out a path to reach your goals. You are able to close the gap between where you are and where you'd like to be because you have a clear vision to move you forward. Being a forward thinker allows you to see the steps needed to get you where you want to go.

**Research** – You enjoy finding information and solutions. Your research abilities help you to identify various options to move your financial agenda forward. You are often the person who saves money by finding a good combination of saving money balanced with good quality purchases. You are discerning when choosing your advisors and understand the options they present as you've done your work to evaluate the alternatives. Your friends may turn to you as a resource as they know you will have reviewed the available options.

**Instincts** – You trust your gut when it comes to making decisions and seeing opportunities. You listen to your inner voice as it warns you of what to avoid and moves you toward situations and people that better serve you.

**Interest** – You're enthusiastic about learning and growing financially. You enjoy learning about concepts and investments. This helps you to make informed decisions. You are curious and ask good questions – often ones that others don't think to ask.

**Action** – Once you have a plan of action, you love to get things done. Given an assignment or task needed to improve your financial situation, you're on it. Smart, informed actions are crucial to being great with money.

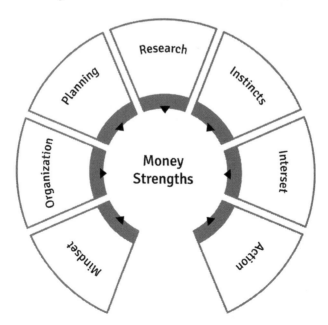

## MESSAGE FROM MONEY

*I see the ways we work well together. Your way is different to others'. I want you to spend more time noticing what you are awesome at when it comes to our relationship. Yes, maybe there are areas in which you can be even better, but let's start at what you already do so well. Yay you!*

### Gain Traction Through Action

What are you great at when it comes to money? Take an inventory of your money strengths. Start with this journal prompt:

*My approach to money is helpful because...*

This is about finding the ways in which you are already great when it comes to money. If you catch yourself focusing on areas in which you feel stuck or less competent when it comes to money, shift your focus back to the ways in which your approach is helpful.

Review the Money Strengths chart above – which areas do you feel strong in? What other strengths did you identify when answering the journaling prompt above?

MONEY MANTRA

**I am already great with Money in many ways.**

## Chapter 8

# Share

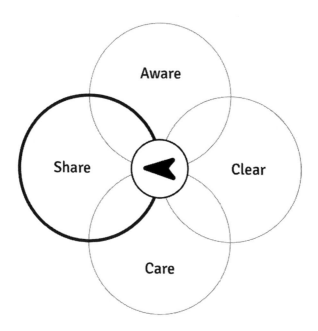

## Loosen Your Grip

When I was a financial advisor and the 2008 recession hit, I saw "natural" instinct kick in as many clung to their money, gripped with the fear they wouldn't be okay. Of course, it wasn't a good idea to be frivolous with spending, but people also stopped giving to causes that were important to them, just when many charities needed support more than ever.

> If you're able to, go ahead and make fists with your hands. Now make them even tighter. What can you receive with fists so tightly closed? This is what it's like to hang on too tightly to what you have.

If you're able to, go ahead and make fists with your hands. Now make them even tighter. What can you receive with fists so tightly closed? This is what it's like to hang on too tightly to what you have. Money loves it when you are generous. It doesn't want you to cling to it too tightly. Money also doesn't want you to give more than is responsible for your financial well-being. Sometimes, people give too much to good causes and family members, leaving their own financial security in jeopardy.

You can begin by sharing small amounts of money. Greg, a successful consultant in financial services, told me how he had been studying the benefits of a regular generosity practice and decided to try an experiment.

He committed to giving at least one dollar to every service provider and unhoused person he encountered in his hometown of Atlanta for the month of February. During this process, he met some wonderful people, had interesting conversations, and felt great. He now continues this practice throughout the year.

Lisa told me about how one year, she decided to say *yes* to every solicitation she was asked for in December. Sometimes, she answered the call with very small amounts of money, and other times with larger amounts, but she said yes to everyone. Lisa felt great not just about helping others, but also doing so during the holiday season when consumerism is at its peak.

Small amounts of money truly make a difference to charities. You might think, what does my $50 contribution do? Certainly large donations from philanthropists such as Mackenzie Scott allow charities to make major investments or start programs, but charities rely on the small donations to keep their programs running.

Why give?

Here's the dirty little secret about generosity. Most people give because it feels good. And there is absolutely nothing wrong with that. If you can make a positive difference for someone else *and* feel great in the process, why not do it more often?

Giving also paradoxically makes you feel wealthier. A study by Zoe Chance and Michael Norton from Harvard Business School suggests that when someone gives to charity, even though their external wealth decreases, they internally feel wealthier. Internally, it might sound like: "If I can give this money away, I must be prosperous."

There are many benefits to be reaped from giving away your time as well as your money. Studies have shown that generous people have greater life expectancies, have better health, and are happier.

## MESSAGE FROM MONEY

*One of the best ways to draw more of me into your life is to share me. When you give, it opens the flow of prosperity. Here's the tricky part: for the most effective results, it's best to do this without an expectation that something will come back to you. It's more of a knowing than an expectation. It is how things work. When you plant quality seeds, water them with kind intentions, and shine love on them, they will sprout. Please experiment with this. Loosen your grip, give me away, see how you feel, and notice what flows to you.*

## Generosity Precedes Prosperity

Don't give back. Yup, I said it. I don't think you should give back. I feel a little cringy when I hear people saying things like, "Now that I'm doing well, I'm giving back." Not that it's bad to want to give; it's that we shouldn't wait.

What if, instead of giving back, you gave *forward*? I constantly witness generosity preceding prosperity in both my personal and my professional life.

When our kids were little, I'd often tell them: "What goes around comes around," meaning *what you put out comes back to you, whether it's good or bad.* And it comes back not necessarily from the person you've given to or in the ways you might expect.

I bet you can think of a time you did something nice for someone, and suddenly, something good happened to you. Sharee shared a story with me about how she was walking in her Chicago neighborhood when a man asked her for some money. Instead of handing him a five-dollar bill, she asked him what he wanted the money

> A simple, effective formula is to give what you want to get, without an expectation of anything in return. If you want more referrals in your business, give more referrals. If you want more love, give more love. Want more money? Be more generous with the money you have.

for. He told her that he tried to clean car windshields for money, but no one would let him that day, and he was hungry. Sharee walked with him to the local grocery store's deli counter and bought him a sandwich.

She felt good that she had helped. That same evening, she received a call from her aunt saying that she and Sharee's uncle wanted to gift her money as part of their estate plan. Boom! Right back at her in a huge and unexpected way. Coincidence? I don't think so. Money tells me over and over that it loves when people share it.

A simple, effective formula is to give what you want to get, without an expectation of anything in return. If you want more referrals in your business, give more referrals. If you want more love, give more love. Want more money? Be more generous with the money you have.

## Gain Traction Through Action

Setting up a systematic giving plan will support you in making generosity a regular occurrence. As you've likely heard, it's good practice to pay yourself first; to take savings off the top of your income and funnel that money into a savings, investment, or retirement account. It's also good practice to establish an automatic giving plan. Here's how it can work:

1. **Decide** on the percentage of your income you'd like to earmark for giving. Using a percentage instead of a fixed dollar amount is a wonderful way to make sure you're giving responsibly; as your income increases,

you're giving more, and if it decreases, you're giving less. What's the right percentage? Well, that's up to you. My husband and I started with 10 percent. That left us with 90 percent of our income for saving and spending. If you have a very high income, perhaps your percentage could be larger. Equally, start with a lower percentage if you're struggling to make ends meet.

**2. Shift** this money into an account earmarked for giving. It can be a simple checking, savings, or money market account to start (larger amounts of money for giving away may require more sophisticated strategies). There are a variety of benefits to starting with this type of account. First, if you end up really needing the money, it's there for you until you've given it away. I suspect you won't use it for anything else, but it may give you peace of mind to know that you could. Next, it will feel less like spending and more like sharing when your contributions come from this giving account, as opposed to straight out of your regular checking account. You'll also know how much you have available to give away, and this will likely inspire you to be more generous with your donations.

**3. Choose** where you'd like to give this money. Find causes, people, and organizations that speak to you. They may be important to you or important to people you love. If your donations go to qualified charities, there may be some tax benefits for you. If you receive a tax deduction, it's as if the government is giving you a bonus for being generous.

**4. Notice** how you feel by setting aside this money and then giving it away. Are you being more deliberate in your giving, knowing what you have available to give away? Are you more generous than you've been in the past?

In the US, the Tuesday after Thanksgiving is called *Giving Tuesday*. It's meant to inspire people to give to charities during the time they are spending on the holidays. What if every Tuesday was Giving Tuesday for you? Or maybe you'd be down for Thoughtful Thursdays! Whether you're focusing on financial giving or doing kind acts for people, be aware of your giving. Set a goal for yourself to do a specific number of kind acts. Five is a good number to start with.

Do you think your happiness levels will increase more from doing *one* kind act a day or doing *five* kind acts in one day? Surprisingly, one study found that happiness levels were higher when five acts of kindness were chunked into one day as opposed to sprinkling them throughout the week!

One way I found helpful to track kind acts is by using an Abundance Activist® wristband. An Abundance Activist is committed to going with the current in their own life and inspiring others to do the same. When I began my process of deliberately upping my generosity, I created wristbands that say "Abundance Activist" on them. Each time I do a kind act, I move the band to the other wrist. A kind act might include contributing to a charity, holding the door open for someone, mentoring, or calling a sick friend. It doesn't have to be donating a kidney! Small acts matter. I give these wristbands away when I speak to groups to encourage this process. You can use a rubber band or a bracelet to track your generosity.

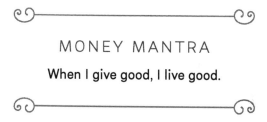

MONEY MANTRA

**When I give good, I live good.**

## Start a Virtuous Cycle

Being generous doesn't typically make sense logically because it comes with a cost in terms of time or money. But, as I mentioned above, it also comes with the benefits of increased happiness, improved health and longevity, and decreased depression.

Generosity is also contagious. Receiving help can motivate us to be generous ourselves. Even watching someone do a kind act can make you feel happier.

I remember being in Trader Joe's one afternoon, and there was an elderly woman in line ahead of me.

As she was checking out, the crew member stopped and said to her: "I'll be right back." I immediately felt impatient and annoyed that I had to wait. Then, he came back with a bouquet of flowers and said to the woman, "I thought you might enjoy these. They are a gift for you." She immediately had a huge smile on her face. When I went to my car, I saw her driving out of the parking lot, still smiling. This small act of kindness made a huge difference to this woman, and when I think about it, I still get a warm feeling in my heart.

My husband and I have used some of the money in our giving account to take volunteer trips with our kids. We've been to a small rural community in Ghana many times. On our first trip, we learned of another volunteer, Kathleen Ismail, who had started a small scholarship fund to provide education for needy and brilliant kids in this area. When she started it, fees were required in Ghana to attend high school. There were many children with bright futures who stopped their education at eighth grade because their families couldn't afford the school fees. Kathleen was compelled to change this for at least some of these kids. Her small NGO has gone on to send 144 children to high school and 87 to university.

When I met Kathleen, I was so inspired by her work that I wanted to support her and get involved in The Ghana Scholarship Fund. Seeing her good work also motivated our family to continue to take trips to the area. Not only did Kathleen's generous spirit spark me to become involved, raise money, and volunteer, it also inspired the scholarship recipients to want to support the community. There are many examples of how these young people have supported the other scholarship recipients and given to their community.

One young woman, Franca, studied accounting at university. After graduation and fulfilling her national service (a requirement in Ghana), she came back to her community to take over managing the library. The Senchi Ferry Library was originally built by Deb McNally, who saw a need in the community. With the support of community leaders, the library team, and dedicated volunteers in the US, Franca has elevated the library to a learning center for both children and adults who want to enhance their reading and computer skills.

Mustapha, the scholarship recipient I mentioned earlier, came from a neighborhood where he was the first to ever go to high school, let alone university. He's been nicknamed "Inspiration." He now volunteers to teach reading and computer skills to people in the community, but by his example alone, he's motivated children to see a bigger future for themselves.

There are many stories of these young people wanting to make a big difference. When I spend time with them, I'm moved to do more to help others.

Closer to home, retail real-estate broker Jacqueline Hayes was so saddened when she saw hungry and unhoused people in the most exclusive areas of

Chicago, she knew she had to help. This was the genesis of The Chicago Help Initiative (CHI). Since their beginnings in 2001, CHI has not only served hundreds of thousands of meals, but supports their guests with programs to find housing, jobs, health-care, and so much more. As a supporter and periodic volunteer for CHI, I'm inspired by what Jackie has started and the impact she's had on the community, the guests, and the volunteers who collaborate with her. The commitment that Jackie brings to her real estate clients, she also brings to her work with CHI. There hasn't been a lunch I've been at with her where she hasn't asked the manager of the restaurant if they could support CHI with a hot meal. One person can impact so many!

## MESSAGE FROM MONEY

I would love you to be a generator of generosity. Know that when you are offering kindness, volunteering your gifts, and sharing me, you are making a positive impact on the world. These acts are like the sun warming all who feel its rays. The more you give, the more warmth you spread. Even a simple smile is contagious. Whose day will you make today? Please take moments to ask: "Who needs my love and support?" Listen to the answer. If no answer comes right away, stay open as you go through your day to notice opportunities for generosity.

## Gain Traction Through Action

**Share your good work with the world.** Sometimes, people are super secretive about their volunteering or generosity. It's admirable to not be doing good work solely to gain recognition, but you might be missing an opportunity to inspire others if you don't talk about your volunteerism. From a business perspective, people want to do business with good people. Being open about the generous work you do can create a halo around you and your business. There are many ways to share about your generosity, including social media, where you might share pictures of you volunteering, tell stories of your experiences, and add your experiences to your bio. Your sincerity will shine through. If you solely talk about volunteering to get more business, people will see this. On the other hand, people will appreciate you sharing your excitement about the ways you support the organizations you work with.

*Journal Prompt: Who needs my support today?*

Tap into your intuition about who you can help. Then act upon these inklings. I've always loved how Benjamin Franklin bookended his days. At the start of each day, he would ask himself: "What good shall I do this day?" At the end of each day, he'd ask: "What good have I done today?" Posting these questions where you can see them serves as another wonderful reminder.

**Ask for donations.** I've had people tell me that they don't feel comfortable asking people to support charities they are involved with because they don't want to obligate their friends and family. The way I see it is that if there is an organization doing good work and I ask people to support them financially, I'm actually helping the person I'm asking. People feel good when they help others. I'm helping people feel good! They may also be getting a tax deduction for their donation, and that's a good thing. I know generosity precedes prosperity, so I'm also helping them to be more prosperous.

**Bring others along to volunteer.** If you volunteer for an organization, invite your friends, coworkers, or clients along. People are often looking for volunteer opportunities and don't know where to contribute their time. At a bank I consult to, we have regular team volunteer events. These support good organizations, make the volunteers feel good, *and* they're a great team-building exercise.

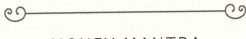

## MONEY MANTRA

I inspire, guide, and awaken goodness in the world.

## Please and Thank You

I was lucky enough to go to overnight camp when I was a child. This was my absolute favorite time of the year. I spent my summers at Camp Birch Knoll for Girls in Northern Wisconsin. One of my first memories of camp was me asking the camp director, Ed, if I could have my turn on the mud slide. This was a very fun and very messy activity that happened after a big rain. I said, "I want to go next!" He looked at me and responded, "CBK girls always say *please* and *thank you*." Boom – lesson learned and not forgotten. It is more than merely being polite. Gratitude brings good things into your life.

Being thankful is simple, yet the many benefits of having a gratitude practice astound me. These include increased happiness, reduced stress, better health, improved sleep, and even reduced inflammation.

Research has also indicated that keeping a gratitude journal can reduce materialism and increase charitable contributions. Materialism (a focus on your belongings) does not make you happier, although at point of purchase, many people likely feel it will. Research suggests that being materialistic without gratitude can lead to *less* life satisfaction. Remember, prosperity is a condition of success and thriving. Prosperity is about more than your possessions.

Even just five minutes a day of focusing on what

you are thankful for can have a significant impact on your well-being.

Money appreciates your appreciation.

Perhaps you already know about the benefits of gratitude and have a regular practice. Are you including gratitude about your financial resources in your daily gratitude? This might sound like:

"I'm grateful for my job and the income it provides to my family."

"I'm grateful for the money I have available to pay

> **Money appreciates your appreciation.**

my rent and have good food in my refrigerator."

"I'm grateful to my parents for teaching me good habits around saving."

"I'm grateful to my company for adding to my pension and retirement plans."

"I'm grateful for finding a quarter on the ground to remind me that abundance is everywhere."

A gratitude practice will make you feel better, and it will also produce practical benefits for your financial well-being. In addition to the decrease in materialism, the reduced stress that can come from gratitude is crucial for sound financial decision-making. Grateful people are nicer to be around, and this is good for your business and career advancement. No one wants to work for an ungrateful jerk, right? Gratitude can build resilience, and the ability to bounce back is important if you experience a financial setback.

When I was a financial advisor, I worked with Carol, who was a very successful realtor. She was wonderful to work with. I'll never forget one of the first meetings I had with her. She teared up as she told me how grateful she was for her clients, her business, and her life. Carol could just as easily have been bitter. She was divorced at an early age and financially responsible for her two daughters. Yet she wasn't bitter. We worked together for many years, and she remained consistently on track for her long-term financial goals and was always one of the top realtors in her community.

After hearing Carol's gratitude, I began to notice how my clients who easily built financial security were all grateful. They focused on what they had with thankfulness. I'd hear comments such as: "It would be nice to update my kitchen, but if it doesn't happen, it will be totally fine. I have a great home." On the other hand, when I'd talk to people who were over-spenders, they would say to me, "I don't drive a fancy car, I don't take big vacations..." They put their attention on what they wanted and didn't have. Remember, one definition of want is *lack*. Focusing on what you don't have is going against the current.

After witnessing gratitude's relationship with financial success, I started a regular gratitude practice with our kids when they were young. Each night before they'd go to sleep, we'd share five things we were grateful for. When I began this nightly ritual, I expected them to say they were grateful for their material possessions like their bicycles or electronics. Instead, I'd hear, "I'm grateful for my friends," "I'm grateful for my teachers," and "I'm grateful that we are happy, healthy and safe."

One night when our son Benjy was about 10 years old, he said to me: "I'm so grateful you and Daddy are so magnanimous, that we live in such a utopia, and that we are so fortuitous." Astounded, I asked him where he learned these words. They were Mrs. Kramer's fifth-grade spelling words that week (full disclosure: I needed spellcheck's assistance to write them out here)!

## MESSAGE FROM MONEY

I am grateful for you. I love the energy you are putting out into the world. I'm excited about being your partner in goodness. Please spend time planning how we can work together to make a wonderful life for you, for those you care about, and for the world you care about. Yes, I know it can feel like a lot sometimes. So much to be done. When we work together, even in small increments, we are changing reality for the better. Please know that I am walking by your side even if you can't see me. I am cheering you on and supporting your good intentions. I really dig it when you notice me and acknowledge the work we are doing together.

## Gain Traction Through Action

What are you grateful for? Try these gratitude practices:

- Before you hop out of bed in the morning, think about five things you are grateful for. As you are thinking about what you are grateful for, tap into the feeling of thankfulness and marinate in these good feelings for a bit.

- Generosity is a physical manifestation of your gratitude. If you're feeling grateful for money in your life, show it by giving some away.

- Journal on gratitude daily. Set a timer for five minutes and write about what you are grateful for. Remember to include gratitude to Money for how it shows up in your life.

- Journal on what you are grateful for that *hasn't* happened yet. Gratitude ahead of results is a lovely way to tap into the feelings of appreciation to propel your goals ahead. Write as if what you desire is already here. For example, "Thank you for the three new ideal clients who have hired me."

- As my editor Emily was taught by her mom, "Give thanks for unknown blessings already on their way!" This phrase comes from Native American wisdom that has stood the test of time. I love the energy of believing good is

coming toward you and being grateful ahead
of time.

- Write "Thank you" under your signature as you
  sign checks or in the memo as you pay bills
  online. You're expressing your gratitude for
  having the funds to pay these bills.

- Send notes of gratitude to people in your life.

- Share what you love and appreciate with
  people in your life. This has become a tradition
  in our family at Friday night dinners.

- Give gifts of gratitude. One year for the holidays, I wrote out what I love and appreciate
  about our kids, my husband, and my mom. I
  printed them out on lovely stationery and had
  them laminated. When my mom passed away, I
  found this among her belongings. It warmed my
  heart to see that she'd appreciated it so much it
  was worth her saving.

- Call someone you haven't talked to in a while
  and share what you appreciate about them.

- Send an "I'm grateful for you" text. Mustapha,
  the young man in Ghana I've mentioned, periodically does this with me. It always brings a big
  smile to my face and inspires me to share my
  gratitude with someone else.

You can bring gratitude and appreciation to your
work in the form of:

- Public appreciation. At a bank I consult with in Chicago, we started a public recognition practice. On a weekly basis, people submit the excellent work they've noticed a team member do. These are summarized and shared with the entire team.

- Sharing individual gratitude. Share your thankfulness for people generously and sincerely. Don't be shy in acknowledging when a job is well done or when someone helps you out. People will appreciate your gratitude when it comes from the heart.

- Gifts of love and appreciation. When I had my financial advisory firm, as I did for my family, I wrote out (and of course laminated!) what I love and appreciate about each of the people who worked with me. I also told them about these things along the way, but having these thoughts documented was well received by them.

It's also helpful to practice gratefully receiving appreciation and recognition from others. If someone is expressing their thankfulness to you and you dismiss it or diminish it by saying, "It was nothing," or, "No problem," it's like throwing their gift back in their face. Responding with a genuine "Thank you" or "My pleasure" will honor their gratitude.

Finally, savor the gratitude you receive. I got the

idea of a "Feel-good file" from Gina Russo, who was the country leader on one of our volunteer vacations. A feel-good file is a physical or electronic file that is used to keep the messages of thanks and acknowledgment you receive. If you have moments of doubt or you feel like you're going against the current, dip into your feel-good file to get a boost. I received a long email from a woman I work with thanking me for the ways she's grown her business, her income, and her happiness. Not only did I put a copy in my feel-good file, I also keep snoozing the email so that it shows up in my inbox every couple of weeks to make me smile!

## MONEY MANTRA

I deserve and welcome the abundance
flowing to me each and every day.
I am grateful for the ways Money shows up for me.

# Now What?

Congratulations! By spending time with Money in the previous pages, you've already started to enhance your relationship with Money. Your commitment to yourself is no small matter.

Keep the momentum going! Continue to build a beautiful relationship with Money and create prosperity on purpose by playing with the practices on a regular basis. Here are three key tactics for keeping up your momentum:

**1. Select a *Money Mantra* for the week** – Select a *Money Mantra* to repeat and review each week. This focus will shift your attention toward creating an even closer relationship with Money and opening your creative energies to build your prosperity. You may choose to fan through the pages, stop when it feels right, and use the *Money Mantra* closest to the page you land on. Or go to www.messagesfrommoney.com/extras to find a listing.

**2. Practice the Prosperity Practices** – Use and review the action steps as your life and situation change. As with exercise, going out for a run once won't keep you in good shape. If you notice yourself going against the current and need a shift, read the *Aware* section and find a Prosperity Practice that feels relevant to you. If you're looking for clarity on your next steps forward, the *Clear* section will help. An annual or biannual review of the *Care* section will help you to be a good partner with Money. And the *Share* section will keep you feeling grateful and abundant and prosperity flowing.

**3. Teach the practices to others** – An effective way to learn new concepts is to share them with other people. You can teach and practice these ideas with your team at work or with your family. For example:

- Explain the idea of going with the current or against the current. How cool would it be to have people in your life experiencing more abundance, positivity, and joy?

- Take moments of silence at the start of team meetings or family get-togethers to build your mindfulness muscles and connection.

- When you hear others using words that go against the current, share the "Cancel/clear away" technique.

- Create a team or family vision for the future, as discussed in the **Clear** section. Work together to imagine it is five years from now; what are you seeing, feeling, experiencing, etc.?

- Have a prosperity-picture party and create visual representations of your future vision.

- Share the concept of a values-based spending plan with your partner and children.

- Establish a group giving plan with family, friends, or coworkers to pool money and funnel it to causes you all care about.

- Share your gratitude on a regular basis with people in your life. You will inspire them to do the same.

- Be an Abundance Activist™ by shifting the conversation from scarcity to abundance. Track your progress with a wristband or bracelet. Notice how many generous acts you do during your day.

You'll find meditations and other resources available for you to continue your journey to creating prosperity on purpose at www.messagesfrommoney.com/extras.

And of course, talk with Money on a regular basis. Money's excited to hear from you!

## MESSAGE FROM MONEY

*I am so grateful for you. I know you are on your path to prosperity. You've already shed many of the limits that have kept us apart in the past. Please know and always remember that I am here for you. Let's have fun together and do meaningful work in the world! I am walking this path with you.*

## MONEY MANTRA

I expect lavish abundance in every aspect of my life. I recognize, welcome, accept, and appreciate lavish abundance, and I am grateful for it.

# Acknowledgments

For me, the acknowledgments section is one of the best parts of writing a book. I love sharing my gratitude memorialized on pages for the people who have been so generous with their encouragement, advice, and support.

Maggie Katz and Gina Calvano were the earliest supporters of my work with Messages from Money. Their encouragement pushed me past my fears and into serving people outside of my immediate network with this work. There would be no book without their support.

A heap of gratitude to Gary Stuart for facilitating the Family Constellations session when Money first let me experience how it's possible for me to be a helpful messenger. He then supported me to step into trusting my intuition at deeper levels.

When I first told my mentor, Peter Cook, about Messages from Money I was a bit worried about what he'd think. He not only leaned in with encouragement but went on to gift messages to important people in his life. I'm so appreciative of this early vote of confidence. And his support helped take my reach to Australia, one of my absolute favorite places.

The very early Monday morning co-writing sessions with Kafi London and Mary Kerrigan helped me to actually get the book finished. Their smiling faces and helpful feedback turned this from a wish to have a book to words on the page.

Thank you to Deb Smolensky for introducing me to the world of mindfulness in business. She brought me to conferences which ultimately led me down the path of being trained by the Search Inside Yourself Leadership Institute. I adore our walking, talking, and creating together.

I am forever grateful for the gentle but strong and consistent pushes from Matt Church, and Lisa O'Neill, my mentors from Thought Leaders Business School. They helped me to move past my fears of seeming like a weirdo in the conservative markets I was used to working in, and step into the power of the teachings and messages Money shares through me. Going public in bigger ways has helped me not only open to more Money Messages but also to serve people around the globe who have learned and grown from these ideas.

A big thank you to Col Fink, my guide and mentor, for encouraging me to write, speak, and teach on my concepts of money and how it works in our lives and businesses. Col, who describes himself as not into "woo," showed me these ideas can inspire and inform many types of people and to get comfortable being "woo AF!"

Kelly O'Malley, Lauren Hawekotte, Miri Upton, Jen Dawson, Jackie Bradley and the other conscious and generous financial advisors and leaders in financial services, I have the honor to work with have shown me the tools and ideas I love to share work in very practical ways. Watching their businesses flourish and grow has been a total joy.

Thank you to Janice Gregory, a brilliant book coach and friend, who from the earliest versions of this book helped to spur creativity and clarity. After each of our conversations, my writing moved ahead much more quickly. It's as if she had her hand on my back helping me to ride up the steep hill with more ease.

I appreciate the guidance and friendship I've received over the years from Tracy Goodheart on how to spread the news about the work that I do. Her expert PR advice and coaching along with her enthusiasm for Messages from Money has helped me immeasurably.

Lynne Twist has been a mentor to me well before I actually met her. Her book, The Soul of Money, changed the entire way I viewed the ways money can work in people's lives. Having the opportunity to get to know her during a women's trip to Ecuador was incredible. She is as brilliant and lovely as I had hoped and more. Thank you for being the inspiration for so many that you are in the world.

I'm so lucky to have found Hambone Publishing in

Australia. Working with the sibling team of Ben and Mish Phillips, and my editor Emily Stephenson made the process feel so much easier. Ben's guidance on the project from start to finish gave me clarity on the process and the confidence we'd have a finished book I could feel great about. Mish understood my work from the very start. Her input on the flow and format was invaluable. Emily was a joy to work with. I *fancy* having such great support in the writing and editing process.

This is the second book project I've worked on with Geoff Affleck. He not only shared his analytical and creative genius about how to serve many with the book, but also held the space for a much bigger reach than I initially had for myself.

And the deepest gratitude goes to the three most important people in my life. Our daughter Amy, our son Benjy, and my husband of oh so many years, Steven. Amy was with me at the beginning of this journey of tapping into my intuition at a deeper level during our trip to the Amazon – our experiences there I believe opened the portal. I adore our travels and time together. Benjy helped me to ground and normalize talking to Money. He said, "That's cool Mom, you're just using your intuition" ... And much gratitude goes to Steven whose support and encouragement have always been a beautiful, generous gift to me.

And to Money...I am very grateful that I'm one of the people you've chosen as a messenger for your wisdom.

# About the Author

Ellen Rogin is a money expert and financial intuitive who helps people transform their relationships with Money so they can have happier, more abundant lives. Her book, *Picture Your Prosperity*, was a New York Times Best Seller, and her work has been featured on CNBC, ABC, NPR, Time, and Oprah Magazine.

As a CPA and CFP®, Ellen worked for many years as a traditional financial advisor before selling her successful wealth management firm. She now combines her intuitive abilities and financial experience to connect with the energy of money and deliver "Messages from Money" to her clients. People worldwide have found her understanding of their relationships with Money to be uncanny.

Ellen's consultations give her clients insight into how to grow their businesses, expand their wealth, and bring an increased sense of peace around money. She is also a sought-after speaker and has trained thousands of conscious financial advisors and entrepreneurs worldwide in the "Art of Prosperity" to grow their businesses and their wealth.

Ellen earned her MBA at NYU Stern School of Business. She now serves on the Board of Directors for The Ghana Scholarship Fund and Metropolitan Capital Bank and Trust.

# About
## *Messages from Money*

I'm passionate about helping to ease suffering around money and enable people to build prosperity.

I do this through my Messages from Money consultations, in which I connect to the energy of money and channel messages meant for my clients. During the consultations, I also rely on the decades of experience I have as a financial advisor to guide my clients in the right direction for their growth.

I've delivered Messages from Money to people worldwide, and their immediate reaction is always the same: they're stunned by what I uncover about their relationships with Money.

But this isn't a party trick. I do this work because most people have a complicated relationship with Money, which causes them all sorts of problems. This can look like worrying they'll lose everything, fighting about money with their partner, or keeping themselves small in their careers.

The Messages from Money consultations often bring immediate clarity to my clients by helping them understand the root cause of their anxieties, frustrations, or money blocks. There's also a healing quality to the work we do together. Sometimes, this happens immediately. Other times, the changes are subtle and take place over many months.

I describe these changes as "Flipping the abundance switch" in your mind. There's a shift that happens during sessions, enabling people to move from a scarcity mindset to one of abundance. As they make this change, my clients dissolve their limiting money beliefs and step into their financial power.

Because of this shift, my clients have been able to:

- Earn more money with ease
- Start charging their worth
- Make strong financial decisions
- Relieve anxiety and confusion about money
- Raise money-smart and well-adjusted kids
- Use money as a force for good.

It is incredibly rewarding to do this work. I love helping people transform their relationships with Money, and I believe the ripple effect will be profound. People will change their lives and the world when they get past the question of "Am I going to be okay?" and instead ask, "How much can I give?"

To learn more and schedule a Messages from Money consultation, go to: www.messagesfrommoney.com.

# What People Are Saying About
## *'Messages from Money'*
### *Consultations*

"Ellen Rogin is that rare financial advisor who can see the big patterns that drive your relationship with money. In her conversations with money session, you will feel truly in touch with what money means and wants for you and what you can do to enhance your relationship with it."

Matt Church, Author of 'Rise Up' and 'Evolution in Leadership,' Founder and Chairperson of Thought Leaders

"I was just sharing about you with a new friend and realized that I had my first session with you and Money a year ago in Feb. As I am just returning down to Earth from a journey in South Africa, I cannot help but be so amused and appreciative of you and everything! Within a three-month period, I visited Egypt and South Africa and had life changing and affirming experiences.
Never would I have dreamt about my recent experiences back last February. I cannot explain where I am now. The only words that I have are 'aligned' and

'abundance.' You and Money are definitely in my angel tribe.

Thank you for being a blessing and sharing your gift with me and the world!"

Tiffany Netters, Consultant

"*Messages from Money* was a game changer for me. The session with Ellen helped me to get clarity around what I needed to do and what I needed to change to realign my relationship with money. Actionable ideas and areas of focus were excellent outcomes – I was expecting money to tell me off but was pleasantly surprised with my reading! Ellen's sessions are excellent, and I highly recommend one for anyone wanting to heal their relationship with money and prosperity."

Lisa O'Neill, CEO of Thought Leaders

"I reflect back on my experience often as a reminder of how money wants to show up in my life. Since that time, money has shifted into such a state of flow and ease in my life. It's so different now than it was before... and it keeps growing and evolving. Before, money was a source of persistent worry (even when I was making money), and now my relationship with money/abundance has completely shifted. It feels like a weight has been taken off my shoulders, and that I've tapped into a source that was always there. Thank you for that beautiful reflection you gave me in that experience!"

James Woeber, Co-Founder and Director at Art of Heartful Living

"I felt truly seen and reassured in my session with Ellen, as if she were channeling messages from money and the universe directly to me. We had never even talked about the details of my financial situation and business; yet she still knew exactly what to ask and provided insightful answers that provided me with great direction. She even shared a Money Mantra with me that was completely aligned with one I'd developed last year and not kept top of mind. Ellen is able to use her considerable gifts of intuition and compassion to create a sense of calm, clarity and abundance in her clients. I highly recommend meeting with Ellen and hearing your own message from Money, if you get the chance to do so. You will not be disappointed!"

Stephanie K. Klein, CEO of Mindfire Mastery

# References

1.  Ariely, Dan. "Predictably Irrational: The Hidden Forces That Shape Our Decisions." Math Comput Educ 44, no. 1 (2010): 68.

2.  Ariely, Dan, and Simon Jones. *Predictably Irrational*. New York: HarperCollins, 2008.

3.  Devanand, C., and Sam Charles. "Behavioral Analysis of Commercial Real Estate Market With Reference to Bangalore." Chief Editor: 55.

4.  Hogue, Timothy. "Abracadabra, or "I Create as I Speak": A Reanalysis of the First Verb in the Katumuwa Inscription in Light of Northwest Semitic and Hieroglyphic Luwian Parallels." *Bulletin of the American Schools of Oriental Research* 381, no. 1 (2019): 193-202.

5.  Newberg, Andrew, and Mark Robert Waldman. *Words Can Change Your Brain: 12 Conversation Strategies to Build Trust, Resolve Conflict, and Increase Intimacy*. Penguin, 2013.

6.  Mullainathan, Sendhil and Eldar Shafir. *Scarcity: Why Having Too Little Means So Much*. New York: Times Books, Henry Holt and Company, 2013.

7.  Newberg, Andrew, and Mark Robert Waldman. *Words Can Change Your Brain: 12 Conversation Strategies to Build Trust, Resolve Conflict, and Increase Intimacy*. Penguin, 2013.

8.  King, Michael Patrick, Director. *Sex and the City, To Market, to Market*. HBO (2003).

9.  Richins, Marsha L., and Scott Dawson. "A consumer values orientation for materialism and its measurement: Scale development and validation." *Journal of Consumer Research* 19, no. 3 (1992): 303-316.

10. Goudreau, Jenna. "Is your partner cheating on you financially? 31% admit money deception." Retrieved January 19, 2023, https://www.forbes.com/sites/jennagoudreau/2011/01/13/is-your-partner-cheating-on-you-financially-31-admit-money-deception-infidelity-red-flags-money-lies/

11. Cameron, Julia, and Mark Bryan. *The Artist's Way*. Sounds True Recordings, 1993.

12. de Montaigne, Michel. "Montaigne's Essays: A Humanistic Approach to Fear." *A Conceptual and Therapeutic Analysis of Fear* (2018): 91.

13. LaFreniere, Lucas S., and Michelle G. Newman. "Exposing worry's deceit: Percentage of untrue worries in generalized anxiety disorder treatment." *Behavior Therapy* 51, no. 3 (2020): 413-423.

14. Predoiu, Radu, Alexandra Predoui, Georgeta Mitrache, Mădălina Firănescu, Germina Cosma, Gheorghe Dinuţă, and Răzvan Alexandru Bucuroiu. "Visualisation techniques in sport–the mental road map for success." *Physical Education, Sport and Kinetotherapy Journal* 59, no. 3 (2020): 245-256.

15. Tseng, Julie, and Jordan Poppenk. "Brain meta-state transitions demarcate thoughts across task contexts exposing the mental noise of trait neuroticism." *Nature Communications* 11, no. 1 (2020): 3480.

16. Garrison, Kathleen A., Thomas A. Zeffiro, Dustin Scheinost, R. Todd Constable, and Judson A. Brewer. "Meditation leads to reduced default mode network activity beyond an active task." *Cognitive, Affective, & Behavioral Neuroscience* 15 (2015): 712-720.

17. Zinsser, William. *On writing well: The classic guide to writing nonfiction*. New York, NY: Harper Collins (2006).

18. Zucker, David and Jerry, and Abrahams, Jim, Directors. *Airplane!* Paramount Pictures (1980).

19. LeBaron-Black, Ashley B., Melissa A. Curran, E. Jeffrey Hill, Russell B. Toomey, Katherine E. Speirs, and Margaret E. Freeh. "Talk is cheap: Parent financial socialization and emerging adult financial well-being." *Family Relations* (2022).

20. Taylor, Tate, Director. *The Help*. Reliance Entertainment and Participant Media (2011).

21. Chance, Zoë, and Michael Norton. "I give therefore I have: Charitable donations and subjective wealth." *ACR North American Advances* (2011).

22. Park, Soyoung Q., Thorsten Kahnt, Azade Dogan, Sabrina Strang, Ernst Fehr, and Philippe N. Tobler. "A neural link between generosity and happiness." *Nature Communications* 8, no. 1 (2017): 15964.

23. Lyubomirsky, Sonja, Kennon M. Sheldon, and David Schkade. "Pursuing happiness: The architecture of sustainable change." *Review of General Psychology* 9, no. 2 (2005): 111-131.

24. Birnbaum, Toby, and Hershey H. Friedman. "Gratitude and generosity: Two keys to success and happiness." Available at SSRN 2398117 (2014).

25. Vogt, Tobias, Fanny Kluge, and Ronald Lee. "Intergenerational resource sharing and mortality in a global perspective." *Proceedings of the National Academy of Sciences* 117, no. 37 (2020): 22793-22799.

26. Musick, Marc A., and John Wilson. "Volunteering and depression: The role of psychological and social resources in different age groups." *Social Science & Medicine* 56, no. 2 (2003): 259-269.

27. Tsvetkova, Milena, and Michael W. Macy. "The social contagion of generosity." *PLOS ONE* 9, no. 2 (2014): e87275.

28. Krull, Kathleen. *Benjamin Franklin*. Penguin, 2013.

29. Watkins, Philip C., Jens Uhder, and Stan Pichinevskiy. "Grateful recounting enhances subjective well-being: The importance of grateful processing." The *Journal of Positive Psychology* 10, no. 2 (2015): 91-98.

30. Emmons, Robert A., and Robin Stern. "Gratitude as a psychotherapeutic intervention." *Journal of Clinical Psychology* 69, no. 8 (2013): 846-855.

31. Redwine, Laura S., Brook L. Henry, Meredith A. Pung, Kathleen Wilson, Kelly Chinh, Brian Knight, Shamini Jain. "Pilot randomized study of a gratitude journaling intervention on heart rate variability and inflammatory biomarkers in patients with stage B heart failure." *Psychosomatic Medicine* 78, no. 6 (2016): 667-676.

32. Jackowska, Marta, Jennie Brown, Amy Ronaldson, and Andrew Steptoe. "The impact of a brief gratitude intervention on subjective well-being, biology and sleep." *Journal of Health Psychology* 21, no. 10 (2016): 2207-2217.

33. Hazlett, Laura I., Mona Moieni, Michael R. Irwin, Kate E. Byrne Haltom, Ivana Jevtic, Meghan L. Meyer, Elizabeth C. Breen, Steven W. Cole, and Naomi I. Eisenberger. "Exploring neural mechanisms of the health benefits of gratitude in women: A randomized controlled trial." *Brain, Behavior, and Immunity* 95 (2021): 444-453.

34. Chaplin, Lan Nguyen, Deborah Roedder John, Aric Rindfleisch, and Jeffrey J. Froh. "The impact of gratitude on adolescent materialism and generosity." *The Journal of Positive Psychology* 14, no. 4 (2019): 502-511.

35. Roberts, James A., Jo-Ann Tsang, and Chris Manolis. "Looking for happiness in all the wrong places: The moderating role of gratitude and affect in the materialism–life satisfaction relationship." *The Journal of Positive Psychology* 10, no. 6 (2015): 489-498.

Made in the USA
Middletown, DE
10 May 2024